COUNTRIES OF THE WORLD

Peru

Gareth Stevens Publishing
A WORLD ALMANAC EDUCATION GROUP COMPANY

About the Author: Janet Heisey traveled in South America for nearly four years and has also traveled extensively in Asia and Europe. She currently lives in New York City and works for the Trickle Up Program, a nonprofit organization dedicated to fighting poverty through microenterprise.

Written by
JANET HEISEY

Edited by
GERALDINE MESENAS

Designed by
JAILANI BASARI

Picture research by
SUSAN JANE MANUEL

First published in North America in 2001 by
Gareth Stevens Publishing
A World Almanac Education Group Company
330 West Olive Street, Suite 100
Milwaukee, WI 53212 USA

For a free color catalog describing
Gareth Stevens' list of high-quality books
and multimedia programs, call
1-800-542-2595 (USA) or
1-800-461-9120 (CANADA).
Gareth Stevens Publishing's
Fax: (414) 332-3567.

© **TIMES MEDIA PRIVATE LIMITED 2001**
Originated and designed by
Times Editions
An imprint of Times Media Private Limited
A member of the Times Publishing Group
Times Centre, 1 New Industrial Road
Singapore 536196
http://www.timesone.com.sg/te

Library of Congress Cataloging-in-Publication Data
Heisey, Janet.
Peru / by Janet Heisey
p. cm. -- (Countries of the world)
Includes bibliographical references and index.
ISBN 0-8368-2333-8 (lib. bdg.)
1. Peru--Juvenile literature. [1. Peru] I. Title.
II. Countries of the world (Milwaukee, Wis.)
F3408.5.H45   2001
985--dc21   00-056348

PICTURE CREDITS
A.N.A. Press Agency: 56 (bottom)
Archive Photos: 14, 15 (bottom), 17, 36, 55, 63, 77, 78, 79, 80, 82
Judi L. Baker: 40
Bes Stock: 3 (top), 45
Michele Burgess: 2, 20, 31, 65, 73, 74, 89
Embassy of Peru: 84
Focus Team: 6, 69
Robert Fried: 4, 28, 32, 34, 83
Eduardo Gil: 9 (top), 10, 21, 26, 35, 41, 42, 44, 46, 53, 56 (top), 72, 75, 87, 91
Haga Library: cover, 1, 3 (bottom), 22, 33, 38, 39, 60
HBL Network: 13, 18, 81
Dave G. Houser: 30, 57, 68
The Hutchison Library: 9 (bottom), 19, 23, 24, 25, 27, 29, 37, 49, 58
North Wind Picture Archives: 11, 15 (top)
Michael J. Pettypool: 16, 51
David Simson: 54
South American Pictures: 5, 7, 8, 12, 43, 47, 48, 50, 52, 59, 61, 62, 64, 66, 67, 71, 76
Tan Chung Lee: 3 (center), 70
Topham Picturepoint: 85

Printed in Malaysia

1 2 3 4 5 6 7 8 9 05 04 03 02 01

Digital Scanning by Superskill Graphics Pte Ltd

Contents

5 AN OVERVIEW OF PERU

6 Geography
10 History
16 Government and the Economy
20 People and Lifestyle
28 Language and Literature
30 Arts
34 Leisure and Festivals
40 Food

43 A CLOSER LOOK AT PERU

44 Andean Music
46 Archaeological Sites
48 Bullfighting
50 Cochineal
52 Cuy
54 El Niño
56 Inca Empire
58 Iquitos
60 Lamoids of Peru
62 Las Huaringas
64 Natural Healers
66 Peruvian Handicrafts
68 Quechua and Aymara
70 Reed Boats
72 Taquile

75 RELATIONS WITH NORTH AMERICA

For More Information ...
86 Full-color map
88 Black-and-white reproducible map
90 Peru at a Glance
92 Glossary
94 Books, Videos, Web Sites
95 Index

AN OVERVIEW OF PERU

With its soaring mountains and pristine lakes, hot deserts and lush jungles, Peru is a country of great diversity. Some of the greatest treasures in the world are found in Peru, and ruins and precious artifacts from great empires abound. Peru was home to one of the world's great civilizations — the Inca Empire. Peru's many different ethnic groups have contributed to its unique culture. People in its urban areas have lifestyles quite different from those in its rural regions. Peruvians living in the jungle, on the coast, and in the mountains also have unique ways of life. Modern Peru, however, faces many problems, such as poverty, inequality, and natural disasters, as it works toward entering the global economy.

Opposite: **University students chat in the Plaza de Armas in the city of Cuzco.**

Below: **Children from the town of Chachapoyas get together for fun and games.**

THE FLAG OF PERU

The national flag of Peru features two vertical bands of red with a white band in the center. White represents peace and justice, while red stands for the blood of those who fought for Peru's independence from Spain. The state, or government, flag (*right*) has the coat of arms of Peru in the center of the white band. The coat of arms consists of a shield framed by a green wreath. It features three items: a vicuña, a relative of the llama; a cinchona tree, the source of quinine; and a yellow cornucopia with gold coins spilling out. These three items represent the country's rich animal, vegetable, and mineral resources.

Geography

Peru is the third-largest country in South America, spanning about 496,225 square miles (1,285,223 square kilometers). Peru borders Ecuador and Colombia to the north, Brazil to the east, Bolivia to the southeast, Chile to the south, and the Pacific Ocean to the west. It has three geographic regions: the coast, the mountains, and the jungle. Peru's capital city is Lima.

Peru has many remarkable geographical features. Lake Titicaca is the world's highest navigable lake at 12,500 feet

LAS HUARINGAS

The lakes in northern Peru are considered sacred. Many Peruvians, together with traditional healers, visit these lakes for healing rituals.
(*A Closer Look, page 62*)

(3,810 meters) above sea level. With a height of 22,205 feet (6,768 meters), Nevado Huascarán is Peru's highest mountain. Colca Canyon is one of the world's deepest canyons, and the Amazon River is the largest river in the world, in terms of volume.

Above: Lima, the capital city of Peru, is the country's center of finance and government. It is a modern and bustling city.

The Coast

The coast is a narrow, lowland desert region, stretching 1,448 miles (2,330 km) along the Pacific Ocean. One of the driest places on the planet, the Peruvian desert coast receives no more than 1 cup (0.25 liter) of measurable precipitation every two years. Rivers run down the mountains, through the desert, and out to the sea, forming small oases, with lush, rich foliage. Human settlement is confined to these river valleys. Three of Peru's major cities, Lima, Trujillo, and Chiclayo, lie in the coastal region.

The Mountains

The Andes mountain chain consists of two parallel ranges that run the length of Peru and separate the coast from the jungle. Both ranges feature snow-covered mountain peaks, some reaching over 20,000 feet (6,096 m). Between the two ranges is a high-altitude, flat grassland area known as the Puna. The eastern edge of the Andes receives more rainfall than the dry

western side. The eastern side has moist, cool cloud forests, as well as tropical rain forests.

Above: **The Amazon rain forest is home to thousands of plant and animal species.**

The Jungle

To the east of the Andes lies the tropical rain forest of the Amazon River basin. Jungle covers 62 percent of Peru's landmass, but few people live in this region. This area contains some of the finest untouched rain forests in the world. Manu National Park, in Madre de Dios, is the most biologically diverse rain forest reserve in the world. It spans 4.5 million acres (1.82 million hectares) and is home to over one thousand species of birds.

The Climate

Just as Peru's geography varies, so does its climate. Each region has different weather patterns, and Peruvians often refer to seasons as "wet" and "dry" rather than winter and summer.

On the coast, the dry season lasts from December to April, when temperatures are about 85°–95° Fahrenheit (29°–35° Celsius). The southern coastal region is one of the driest places on Earth. Since rain-bearing winds from the Amazon basin are blocked by the Andes, very little rain falls in this area. In the mountains, the dry season lasts from May until September, with cool nights and little rain. This period is generally considered the summer season in the Andes. The period from October to April is the winter season, when the region receives a large amount of rainfall. In the jungle, the wet season lasts from January through April, when heavy rains fall, sometimes causing landslides. The jungle also receives rain during the dry season, but not as frequently or as heavily.

Every few years, a phenomenon known as El Niño occurs. Weather patterns become erratic, and the country is subjected to heavy rains and floods in some areas and drought in others.

EL NIÑO

The climate in Peru is disrupted once every few years by a phenomenon known as El Niño. El Niño brings torrential rains, floods, and drought to different parts of the country. *(A Closer Look, page 54)*

Left: People in the jungle region live in houses on stilts. These stilts keep houses dry during the floods of the wet season.

Opposite, bottom: The giant *Puya raimondii* takes almost one hundred years to grow to full size and flower. After flowering just once, however, the plant dies.

8

Left: The toucan, with its distinctive multi-colored beak, is one of the many species of birds that inhabit the Amazon rain forest.

LAMOIDS OF PERU

Llamas and alpacas, two members of the lamoid family, have been domesticated by Peruvians for centuries. They serve as pack animals and provide wool and meat for Peruvians. Vicuñas and guanacos, also lamoids, live in the wild.
(*A Closer Look, page 60*)

NATURAL HEALERS

Modern scientists are gradually discovering the medicinal properties of the plants in the Amazon rain forest, a knowledge jungle tribes, such as the Machiguenga, have had for a long time.
(*A Closer Look, page 64*)

Plants and Animals

Peru has a tremendous variety of plant and animal life. One of the most famous animals in Peru is the condor, the largest flying bird in the world. Condors have wing spans of up to 10 feet (3 m) and are carrion feeders, eating the carcasses of dead animals. They can soar to altitudes of 20,000 feet (6,096 m) in search of food.

Lamoids, relatives of the camel family, roam throughout the Andes mountains. Members of the lamoid family include llamas, alpacas, vicuñas, and guanacos. The spectacled bear lives in Peru's cloud forests and is nearly the same size as the North American black bear. The spectacled bear eats plants, large insects, and small animals.

The Amazon area is a tropical rain forest rich in plant and animal life. Almost half the 1.6 million species of animals known to live on Earth are found in the rain forest, including jaguars, sloths, deer, and many species of monkeys. Of the nearly one thousand species of birds in the rain forest, some of the most familiar are parrots, macaws, parakeets, and toucans. The rain forest also has a large variety of plant and insect life.

One plant unique to the Andes is the giant *Puya raimondii*. This plant is a member of the pineapple family and looks like a cactus. It takes nearly one hundred years to grow to full size. It then flowers by producing a huge spike up to 30 feet (9 m) in height and covered with flowers.

History

The first Peruvians probably came from Asia in about 1250 B.C. They settled in small groups and lived by hunting and fishing. Each group formed a distinctive society, and many cultural groups developed in different regions. Some early societies in Peru included the Chimú, the Chavín, and the Nazca. Perhaps the best known ancient society in Peru was the glorious Inca Empire, which reigned from 1438 to 1532.

The Inca Empire

The Incas began as a society in central Peru in the twelfth century. By 1438, under the reign of Pachacuti, the Inca Empire was a highly developed and sophisticated civilization. The Incas had exceptional organizational skills. With a huge work force and incredible coordination, the Incas irrigated deserts and mountaintops, constructed a vast infrastructure of roads, and built tremendous warehouses and temples.

The Arrival of the Spaniards

Around 1525, the Incan leader Huayna Capac died, leaving two sons, Atahuallpa and Huascar, to battle for control of the empire. The civil war that followed weakened the Inca Empire and made

ARCHAEOLOGICAL SITES

Peru's landscape is dotted with ruins and wonders left by many ancient societies. Two of the most famous archaeological sites are the tombs near the village of Sipán and the giant line drawings in Nazca.
(A Closer Look, page 46)

INCA EMPIRE

At its height, the Inca Empire stretched from south of modern-day Colombia to Chile. This enormous empire, however, lasted less than one hundred years — from about 1438 to 1532.
(A Closer Look, page 56)

Left: **On November 16, 1532, the Spaniards kidnapped Atahuallpa, who was then the Incan ruler, and imprisoned him. The Spaniards asked Atahuallpa's people to pay a huge ransom in gold and silver for his release. After the ransom was paid, however, the Spaniards realized that the powerful Atahuallpa would be a threat to them if they released him. In 1533, the Spaniards executed Atahuallpa.**

the Incas easy targets for a small group of Spaniards who arrived in Peru in 1532. The Spaniards, led by Francisco Pizarro, desired the Incas' gold and silver treasures. Using horses and guns, the Spaniards fought the Incas, who were equipped only with stones and lances.

In 1533, the Spanish executed the last Incan ruler, Atahuallpa, and the Inca Empire was defeated by 1535. The Spaniards then named Lima the capital city of Peru. The indigenous people and African slaves were forced to mine silver and gold, all of which was sent to the Spanish king. Thousands of slaves died in this endeavor. Many people in Spain, including some members of the Spanish clergy, protested the cruel treatment of the native and African peoples, but Spanish leaders in Peru did not listen. In 1781, Túpac Amaru II, a descendant of Atahuallpa, attempted a revolt against the Spanish rulers, but he was captured and killed.

Opposite: **The magnificent fortress of Sacsayhuamán, situated near the Incan capital of Cuzco, is the site of many important Incan festivals. Experts estimate that tens of thousands of laborers took seven decades to complete this massive fortress.**

The Fight for Independence

On July 28, 1821, Peruvians, now a mixture of indigenous people and Peruvian-born Spaniards, declared their independence from Spain. Their struggle to be free of Spanish rule continued, however, until 1824, when Peru, with the assistance of armies from Venezuela and Chile, finally defeated the Spanish.

Politics and Economic Development

Peru's economy developed rapidly in the late nineteenth century. The construction of a railroad system that connected the various regions helped bring the riches of the jungle regions to the coast for export. As the economy boomed in the early 1900s, foreigners established mining companies, factories, fish meal plants, and sugar plantations.

Problems in politics and international relations arose during the second half of the nineteenth century. In 1864, Peru fought with Spain over control of the guano-rich Chincha islands. In 1879, Peru and Bolivia fought a territorial war against Chile, called the War of the Pacific. The Chileans won control over a large part of southern Peru.

From 1900 to 1950, Peru had eighteen presidents, many of whom were dictators who practiced repressive rule. In the mid-1920s, workers in the mines, factories, and plantations organized

IQUITOS

Iquitos, the capital city of the department of Loreto, was the center of an international rubber boom, which occurred between 1883 and 1912.
(*A Closer Look, page 58*)

Left: **During the rubber boom of the 1890s, many indigenous people were employed as rubber tappers. They were paid very poorly and were treated badly.**

12

Left: Soldiers search voters during the 1990 election in an attempt to prevent riots and terrorist activities that were common in the 1980s.

labor unions to improve working conditions. In 1924, political activist Victor Raúl Haya de la Torre formed the American Popular Revolutionary Alliance (APRA), which protested the mistreatment of workers and fought for the nationalization of industry. Haya de la Torre was defeated in the 1931 election, but APRA continues to be a significant opposition party today.

Political and economic instability in Peru continued into the second half of the twentieth century, in spite of numerous attempts at reform. The governments were alternately dictatorships and democracies. Fernando Belaúnde Terry was president from 1963 to 1968 and from 1980 to 1985. During his first term of office, he brought about reforms in public works and improved social benefits. His government also settled a dispute with foreign investors over Peruvian oil fields.

The armed forces ousted him in 1968, and General Juan Velasco Alvarado took control in 1970. Velasco's government seized foreign-owned ranches, imposed price controls on basic goods and services, and instituted sweeping land reforms. His large-scale construction projects and attempts to suppress the production of coca led to more political and economic crises. In 1985, an APRA candidate, Alan García Pérez, came to power, but he also failed to establish economic and political stability in Peru.

Sendero Luminoso

In the 1980s, a revolutionary group known as *Sendero Luminoso*, or Shining Path, began a terrorist movement against the elected government. Members of this movement believed true reform in Peru could only be achieved through revolution. Government offices were bombed, and local officials were killed in terrorist activities that lasted twelve years. In 1992, the group's power was undermined when its leaders Víctor Polay Campos and Abimael Guzmán Reynoso were arrested.

Fujimori and Peru Today

In 1990, Alberto Fujimori was elected president in a surprise victory. Within months, he imposed strict reforms to stabilize the economy. In 1993, he dissolved the constitution, the Congress, and the judiciary, because he felt they blocked his reform efforts. After Fujimori was reelected in 1995, he made further changes in the constitution and restored Peru's relations with international partners. By the end of the century, Peru had developed a stronger economy and enjoyed good relations with other nations, but President Fujimori's severe economic measures also left many Peruvians unemployed or underemployed.

Below: **President Fujimori (*center*) received a decoration from President Jamil Mahuad Witt (*right*) of Ecuador during a visit to Ecuador in October 1999.**

Atahuallpa (1502–1533)

Atahuallpa, the last Incan ruler, was the son of Incan ruler Huayna Capac and an Ecuadorian princess. Huayna Capac died in 1525, and the kingdom was divided between Atahuallpa and his half brother, Huáscar. Atahuallpa soon fought his brother for control over the empire. Atahuallpa eventually defeated his brother in 1532, but the civil war weakened the Incan kingdom and made it an easy target for the Spaniards, who arrived at this time. The Spaniards kidnapped Atahuallpa, demanding a huge ransom in gold and silver for his release. After receiving the ransom, however, the Spaniards did not release Atahuallpa. On August 29, 1533, the Spaniards executed Atahuallpa.

Atahuallpa

Andrés Avelino Cáceres (1833–1923)

Andrés Avelino Cáceres, the president of Peru from 1886 to 1890, was a commander during the War of the Pacific against Chile. After Chile conquered the city of Lima in 1881, he fled to the highlands and formed a peasant resistance movement. He then mounted a revolt in the capital. According to legend, Cáceres lost many men during the revolt, but as Chilean forces approached, he led his men and a large herd of llamas to the top of a cliff. He hoped that the Chileans would not be able to tell the difference between man and beast. The Chileans fled, thinking themselves outnumbered.

Javier Pérez de Cuéllar (1920–)

A well-known diplomat and ambassador, Javier Pérez de Cuéllar was born in Lima on January 19, 1920. He joined the foreign ministry in 1940 and the diplomatic service in 1944, serving in embassies in France, Britain, Bolivia, and Brazil. Pérez de Cuéllar became Peru's first ambassador to the Soviet Union in 1969. On January 1, 1982, he was appointed the secretary-general to the United Nations. In 1986, he was reelected to the same post. Pérez de Cuéllar is credited with ending the Iran-Iraq War through negotiations in August 1988. In 1995, he ran for the presidency in Peru but was defeated by Alberto Fujimori.

Javier Pérez de Cuéllar

Government and the Economy

Peru is a republic. It is divided into twenty-four departments, plus the constitutional province of Callao, which has some of the functions and rights of a department. Each department is governed by a regional assembly. All the departments and Callao report to the central government in Lima.

Under the constitution of December 1993, the president is the head of the executive branch. He or she is elected for a five-year term and may seek reelection for an additional five years. The legislative branch of the government consists of the Congress, which has 120 seats. Members are elected by popular vote to serve five-year terms. Supreme Court judges are appointed by the National Council of the Judiciary and are the highest judicial authority in the land.

Voting in Peru is compulsory for men and women between the ages of eighteen and seventy.

Left: **The impressive changing-of-the-guards ceremony at the palace in Lima is held daily.**

Left: **Peruvian special commandos, who rescued hostages during the siege of the Japanese embassy in Lima, honor their fallen comrades at a ceremony held on April 22, 1998.**

President Fujimori and His Reforms

In 1992, President Fujimori effectively closed down the government of Peru. He dissolved Congress and dismantled the judicial system. After ruling the country as a dictator, he then organized the rewriting of the constitution, implemented in 1993, and reestablished the judiciary system. Elections were held in 1995 for a new Congress.

Fujimori changed the law so that he could run for a third term in 2000. He won reelection, but the opposition parties accused Fujimori of rigging the vote. Soon after, when criticism of the election continued and Fujimori's security chief was accused of corruption, Fujimori announced that a new election would be held and that he would not run again.

The Military

Peru's military force numbers 125,000. Peru also has a special anti-terrorism force. Its skill became known internationally during the siege of the Japanese ambassador's residence in Lima in 1997. Terrorists held seventy-two hostages there for nearly four months until the anti-terrorism squad ambushed the residence, freeing all but one of the hostages. Two soldiers and all fourteen terrorists were killed.

Industry

Mining is one of Peru's primary industries, and copper mines employ a large portion of the labor force. The petroleum industry is also important, with most operations based in jungle regions and on the northern coast. Other major industries include building materials, chemicals, electronic products, food processing, pharmaceuticals, plastic products, and textiles. Almost 70 percent of Peru's industry is concentrated in the Lima metropolitan area.

Agriculture and Fishing

Approximately one-third of Peru's population works in agriculture and fishing, although these industries contribute a relatively small amount to the country's gross domestic product (GDP). Peru is one of the top five harvesters of fish in the world, with anchovies and pilchards the most common types of fish caught. Large quantities of fish meal are produced and sold for use as livestock feed.

In agriculture, the main commercial crops are rice, sugarcane, corn, and cotton. Many crops are grown to feed the

COCHINEAL

The cochineal, a small insect that grows on the prickly pear cactus, produces carmine. Carmine, a red dye, provides a good source of income for Peruvians living in the desert.
(A Closer Look, page 50)

Below: **Salt is produced on ancient Incan terraces.**

local population, including potatoes, corn, wheat, vegetables, and fruit. The main agricultural export crop is officially coffee, but Peru earns large amounts of money from the export of coca, a plant that is the raw material used in the production of cocaine.

Natural Resources

Peru has tremendous natural resources, ranking among the world's top ten producers of silver, copper, lead, and zinc. Peru's jungle regions, which account for over 60 percent of its landmass, provide a wealth of resources such as oil, rubber, and wood, including a large proportion of Peru's valuable hardwood. Large oil deposits are found on the northern coast of Peru, and natural gas production is based in the central part of the lowlands. Fish reserves are dwindling, but Peru remains the world's largest producer of fish meal.

MAIN IMPORTS AND EXPORTS

Peru's main imports include cereals and other foodstuffs, machinery, transportation equipment, and manufactured goods. Copper is the country's most important export, but world copper prices have declined recently, affecting export revenues. Other mineral exports include petroleum products, zinc, gold, lead, and silver. Peru's biggest trading partners, both for imports and exports, are the United States and Japan.

People and Lifestyle

The Indigenous People of Peru

Indigenous people make up the largest portion of the Peruvian population — about 45 percent. In general, the indigenous people of Peru occupy the lowest socioeconomic level. Some indigenous people speak only their native language — Quechua, Aymara, or one of the many tribal languages. Some people in the smaller tribes cannot speak Spanish and are therefore often left out of the mainstream economy. The literacy rate for Peru's indigenous people is the lowest of any comparable group in South America.

The two largest indigenous groups are the Aymara in the southeast and the Quechua, a much larger group living throughout the country but primarily in the mountains. Approximately 200,000–250,000 Amazon Indians from about fifty ethnic groups live in scattered communities in the jungles of Peru. Other indigenous groups living in the jungle include the Yaguas and Jivaros in the Amazon Basin and the Machiguenga and Yaminahua in Manu National Park.

QUECHUA AND AYMARA

The Quechua and Aymara are the largest groups of indigenous people in Peru. Many have preserved their traditions in their clothing, handicrafts, and food.
(*A Closer Look*, page 68)

Below: Peru's indigenous people celebrate a religious festival in Cuzco.

TAQUILE

The island of Taquile lies on Lake Titicaca. Increasing numbers of tourists flock to the island every year, but the people of Taquile remain traditional in their dress and customs.
(*A Closer Look, page 72*)

AFRICAN-PERUVIANS

In the sixteenth century, the Spaniards brought thousands of slaves from Africa to work in the new colonies. Unlike in other parts of the Americas, slaves in Peru arrived in small groups from many different geographic locations in Africa. The Spaniards' intent was to reduce the chance of revolt among the slaves by ensuring that there were no common leaders and no common languages. As a result, the African population in Peru is more diverse than in other parts of the Americas. Most Peruvians of African descent live on the country's coast.

Each tribe is unique. Although many tribes have changed drastically over the years due to contact with the outside world, a few have maintained their culture and identity.

Other Ethnic Groups

The second largest population group is the *mestizos* (mess-TEEZ-ohs), who are of mixed indigenous and European ancestry. They account for 37 percent of the population. Caucasians make up 15 percent of the population. The remaining 3 percent of the population consists of Africans, Japanese, Chinese, and other groups. Asians, mostly from Japan and China, first arrived in Peru in the nineteenth century to work as laborers on railways and plantations. The Asian population currently has a very high-profile representative; Alberto Fujimori, the president of Peru since 1990, is of Japanese descent.

Family Life

The extended family is very important in Peru, just as it is in most of South America. Peruvian families make decisions together and discuss all family issues. Close family members include aunts; uncles; cousins, who are often called brothers and sisters; and grandparents. Close friends of the family and godparents of the children are often called aunts or uncles and form a part of the extended family as well. These are the people with whom a Peruvian will spend most of his or her time.

Children are included in nearly all daily activities. On the rare occasions that parents are away, other family members usually look after the children.

Unlike in some countries, Peruvian teenagers are not encouraged to be independent and to leave the family home upon starting college or work. Instead, it is generally expected that children will stay with their families until they have a family of their own. Teenagers are taught to value their families and are

REED BOATS

Fishermen in Huanchaco and on the Uros Islands use boats made entirely of reeds. In fact, buildings on the Uros Islands and the very islands themselves are made of reeds.
(*A Closer Look, page 70*)

Below: **Extended families in Peru get together for many activities. This extended family is having refreshing fruit on a hot, sunny day.**

generally given support and guidance throughout their lives. Young adults continue to live with their parents until they are married, and a married couple often lives with one set of parents until the newlyweds can afford to rent or buy their own home. This is done not only for economic reasons, but also because the family is considered an individual's greatest strength.

Above: **This Quechua bridal couple performs traditional wedding rituals in Cuzco.**

Gender Roles

The roles of men and women in Peruvian society remain traditional. Women and girls are generally responsible for the maintenance of the household, while men and boys work outside the home to generate income for the family. As families begin to require two incomes to survive, more women are taking jobs outside the home. They often remain in lower-level jobs, however, and are still expected to perform their traditional roles at home.

Education

Education is free and compulsory for children six to twelve years of age. Secondary school, for children from ages twelve to fifteen, is not compulsory and is not well attended. Fewer than half of the children eligible for this level of education are actually enrolled in school.

Children attend school from Monday to Friday and have a three-month vacation during the summer season, which starts in December. Most schools teach classes in Spanish, but some schools in the rural areas include instruction in the local language as well. The literacy rate of Peruvians is rising, and today, 88.7 percent of the population over the age of fifteen can read and write. The number of women without the ability to read and write, however, is much higher than the number of men.

A great deal of difference exists between education in Peru's urban areas and education in its rural regions. In cities, school attendance is generally more strictly enforced, and parents are contacted if children are gone from school for an extended period

Below: **A teacher instructs a group of students in a school near Cuzco.**

of time. In rural areas, however, children often do not attend school regularly because they are needed at home to help work in the fields or care for their siblings.

Higher Education

Peru has over forty public and private universities and two Catholic universities. The National Autonomous University of San Marcos, established in 1551, was the first university founded in the Americas.

Many of Peru's universities are in Lima, but twenty of the twenty-four departments also have universities because the demand for higher education is quite high. University graduates are well respected in Peru. Regardless of their degree or course of study, graduates are addressed as "doctor" or "professor" as a sign of respect. In villages and towns, graduates are often approached to resolve disputes. For Peruvian women, pursuing an education is one way to achieve higher social standing and increased respect as an individual.

Catholicism

The Spaniards brought the Catholic faith to Peru. Today, most Peruvians are Catholic, and Catholic holidays are observed in the country. Non-practicing Catholics also often participate in the rituals of the church, choosing to be married by a priest or having their children baptized. In 1965, the Roman Catholic Church stopped requiring that Masses be held in Latin, and today, Masses in Peru are held in Spanish, Quechua, and Aymara. Church officials have also moved toward working more closely with communities to help solve their members' problems.

Missionaries

Mormons and other Protestants are gaining prominence in Peru because of the increased work of missionaries. Missionaries have been present among jungle populations for a long time, but recently the number of missionaries has increased on the coast and in the mountains of Peru. Most of these missionaries represent groups based in North America.

Left: **After the Spaniards arrived in Peru, missionaries helped spread the Catholic faith throughout the country.**

Indigenous Beliefs

Many people in the highlands of Peru practice a traditional form of religion that worships natural elements as spiritual beings. This religion dates back to the time before the Spaniards arrived and is possibly a mixture of the traditions of the Incan and pre-Incan societies. The Spaniards denounced these beliefs, declaring that they amounted to devil-worship. The native populations, however, found ways to practice their religion and included Catholic saints among their own gods. For example, Christian-looking crosses that sit on top of many hills and mountains in Peru represent *apus* (AH-poohs), or mountain spirits.

APUS AND PACHAMAMA

Peru's indigenous people believe that each mountain is a spirit, or apu. Apus are the givers of life and controllers of nature and destiny. Mountains have the power to bring water or drought, storms or fair weather. Villagers make regular offerings to the apus to worship and appease them. Piles of stones are often found along mountain trails. Each traveler who passes places another stone on top of the pile, to ask the apus for safe passage. Villagers who sit and rest on the mountainside often place three good coca leaves, in the pattern of a flower, into a protected spot on the mountain — behind a rock or in a hole — as an offering to the apu. When taking a sip of a drink, Peruvians often spill the first few drops on the ground as an offering to Pachamama, or Mother Earth.

Language and Literature

A variety of languages are spoken in Peru. The three most common languages spoken are Spanish, Quechua, and Aymara. Spanish and Quechua are the official languages in Peru.

Spanish was introduced in South America by Spanish conquerors in the sixteenth century, and it is now spoken by most people in Peru. For many Peruvians, Spanish is the language spoken outside the household, while Quechua, Aymara, and other local languages are often used within the family. A small percentage of Peru's population cannot speak Spanish. These people usually live in isolated areas in the Andean highlands or in the jungle, where contact with Spanish speakers is limited.

Quechua is an ancient language most closely associated with the Incan dynasty. Various tribes in southern Peru spoke Quechua before the Incas adopted it as the official language. When the Incas conquered these tribes, they established Quechua as the

Below: Bookstands are a common sight along streets in Lima.

28

Left: Mario Vargas Llosa is the most famous author in Peru. He was born in Arequipa but moved to Europe after completing college. He lived in Europe for sixteen years but continued to write about and visit Peru during that time. His novels include *Aunt Julia and the Scriptwriter*, *The War at the End of the World*, and *Conversations in the Cathedral*. In 1990, Vargas Llosa ran for the presidency of Peru as the candidate of the conservative Libertad (Liberty) party. He lost the election to Alberto Fujimori. Following his defeat, Vargas Llosa returned to Europe and became a Spanish citizen. He maintains a double citizenship, Peruvian and Spanish, and continues to write.

official language to draw the tribes into the empire. By the time the Spaniards arrived in 1532, Quechua was the principal language spoken in Peru. Spanish spread rapidly after the Inca Empire fell.

The Aymara language comes from a society known as the Tiahuanaco, which existed from 200 B.C. to A.D. 1200. Some linguists believe that Quechua and Aymara may have descended from the same language but developed as two distinctly different languages. The majority of Aymara speakers live in the area around Lake Titicaca, near Bolivia.

Peruvian Literature

Early writers, such as Garcilaso de la Vega and Huamán Poma de Ayala, chronicled events that took place during the Spanish conquest of Peru. Other Peruvian authors have contributed to South American literature. César Vallejo (1892–1938), considered one of the twentieth century's greatest poets, chose poverty and social injustice as his central themes. Ciro Alegría (1909–1967) was one of the first to write about the experiences of the indigenous people of Peru.

Flora Tristan (1803–1844) was a vocal supporter of women's and workers' rights in Peru, although she lived outside of Peru much of her life. She visited Peru in the 1830s. Her book *Peregrinations of a Pariah* is a tribute to the women of Lima, whom she saw as highly independent.

Arts

Before the Spanish arrived, the main forms of artistic expression were ceramics and textiles. They are believed to contain themes and messages for communicating in place of a written language. Much of what historians know of the pre-Columbian cultures in Peru has come from studies of these art forms.

Ceramics

The ancient Moche society made ceramics that showed realistic scenes of daily life and portrayed facial features with great clarity. Moche ceramics show people playing music, making pottery, building temples, and tending crops, revealing the types of crops they grew. The ceramics also portray human beings in many different states — wealthy, poor, happy, and mournful.

Textiles

People of the ancient Nazca and Paracas societies were experts in weaving and making textiles. Their textiles are among the finest examples of weaving discovered anywhere in the world. Artists used up to 190 shades of color, and an extremely tight weave enabled them to use tremendous detail. These textiles feature a variety of subjects taken from the lives of the people.

Left: Peruvians are very artistic people, and many produce handicrafts for sale to tourists. This vendor sells her wares at Ollantaytambo.

Left: **This woman weaves beautiful belts and scarves for sale at the crafts market in Chincheros.**

PERUVIAN HANDICRAFTS

The growth in tourism has helped Peru's handicrafts industry survive and grow. Peruvian ceramics and textiles are some of the most popular craft items among tourists.
(*A Closer Look, page 66*)

Weavers today are rediscovering ancient weaving techniques. The tourist industry has helped their business grow and given them a greater impetus to discover the ancient weavers' secrets.

Painting

Peruvian painting developed after the arrival of the Spaniards. The most famous painters emerged from the Cuzco School, a group of indigenous painters who had been taught by Spanish artists. Spanish and Italian instructors brought paintings from Europe for Peruvian painters to study, but the Peruvian students injected indigenous elements into their paintings. Marcos Zapata's famous painting of the Last Supper in the Cuzco Cathedral features Jesus and his apostles feasting on Andean cheese, hot peppers, and guinea pig!

Architecture

Architectural styles vary considerably among regions in Peru. Old and new styles blend in Lima, where modern buildings and hotels stand alongside Spanish colonial buildings. The city of Arequipa also has beautiful colonial architecture.

The city of Cuzco is a fascinating blend of Spanish and Incan architecture. Incan stonemasons were very skilled. Their knowledge of the principles of engineering remains unparalleled in modern society. Stones used to construct buildings were skillfully carved and shaped and then placed carefully on top of one another, without mortar or other materials to hold them

Below: **Many buildings in Cuzco feature ancient Incan stonework at the base of their walls.**

together. The stones were placed with such accuracy that, even today, the blade of a knife cannot be inserted between any two stones. The walls of Incan buildings sloped slightly inward to protect them from damage during an earthquake. The Spaniards built on top of Incan foundations. When earthquakes occurred, the Spanish additions were often destroyed, while the Incan foundations remained intact.

Music

Each cultural group in Peru has contributed to the country's rich musical diversity. Among the most popular musical forms are *huayno* (WHY-no), a rural, indigenous form of music, and *saya* (SIGH-ah). Andean folk music is also very popular.

The African-Peruvian musical tradition is very strong, particularly on the coast. *Criollo* (cree-OY-oh) is a combination of African rhythms and European phrasing. Many Afro-Peruvian performers have become internationally famous, including Chabuca Granda and Susana Baca. These two singers regularly perform in Peru and all over the world.

Chicha (CHEE-chah) mixes the criollo and Andean styles. Peruvians also enjoy merengue and salsa, lively forms of dance music popular throughout South America. *Salsatecas* (sahl-sah-

ANDEAN MUSIC

Andean folk music is very popular in Peru. Andean music features wind and string instruments, such as the *zampoña* (zahm-POHN-yah) and the harp.
(A Closer Look, page 44)

TAY-cahs), nightclubs that play salsa music, are popular, especially in large cities. Rock and pop music in English and Spanish are also popular.

Above: **Dancing livens up many celebrations and festivals in Peru. These Quechua Indian children perform during Inti Raymi, the Incan New Year.**

Dance

Peru's National Ballet performs in Lima. The country's folk dancers represent Peru at many international dance and folkloric competitions and events. These dancers combine the numerous styles of dance in Peru. Many of the dancers belong to troupes that perform ancient, traditional dances in celebration of annual harvests or religious events.

Leisure and Festivals

Leisure Activities

People living in Peru's major cities enjoy going to the movies, shopping, playing games in video arcades, and dining out. From December to March, the summer season on the coast, the beaches fill with people swimming, surfing, and playing in the sand.

Peruvians everywhere like to *dar un paseo* (DAHR UN pah-SAY-oh), or take a walk, in the evenings, generally around the town square. No matter what the size of the city or village,

Below: **On weekends, Peruvians enjoy browsing at flea markets, such as this one in Lima.**

at about 7:00 p.m., the main plaza fills with families, couples, teenagers, and children strolling, sitting, and chatting with one another. Children in cities also enjoy skateboarding. Peruvians are very sociable people, and they enjoy visiting with their families and friends.

Television is popular with many Peruvians, and they watch programs from all over South America. Favorite T.V. programs include sports programs, especially soccer, and *telenovelas* (tay-lay-noh-VAY-lahs), or soap operas. In villages where electricity is expensive or not available to everyone, the municipality will install a television set in the main plaza. In cities and towns, people without televisions gather outside electronics shops to watch their favorite programs on display sets.

Dancing is a favorite pastime all over Peru. Salsa and merengue music are preferred for dancing in the coastal cities, while huayno music is popular in the highlands.

Social Interaction

Peruvians enjoy being with friends and family. Whether taking a walk, watching television, or listening to music, members of the extended family will almost always be included. In more remote areas and traditional indigenous communities, families use

Below: **Young skateboard enthusiasts meet regularly to learn new skateboarding techniques and have fun with others sharing the same interest.**

leisure time to instruct their children about their history, culture, and legends.

Sapo

A traditional game played in some parts of Peru is *sapo* (SAH-poh), or toad. It is often played at restaurants or in taverns. In sapo, a metal toad sits on top of a box that has holes cut into it. Each hole has a point value assigned to it. Players throw metal disks at the sapo and try to get them into the sapo's mouth to earn the most points or in one of the holes for a lesser number of points. The player with the most points wins.

Soccer

Soccer is one of the most popular sports in Latin America, and Peru is no exception. Peru has many soccer teams. Some of the best teams in Lima include Universitario de Deportes, Alianza Lima, and Sporting Cristal. The Peruvian national soccer team plays in international tournaments.

One of the most famous soccer players in Peru is Teófilo Cubillas. Cubillas scored more goals for the Peruvian national team than any other Peruvian. At the age of sixteen, Cubillas started playing soccer professionally as a forward for Alianza Lima. He later joined the Peruvian national team and played in the 1970 World Cup in Mexico. Peru advanced to the later rounds in that tournament, and Cubillas scored five goals in four games. He played in the World Cup tournament again in 1978. In all, Cubillas scored ten goals in World Cup tournaments and remains among the top ten players in total goals scored in World Cup matches. He went on to play soccer in Europe and the United States and now coaches the sport in Miami, Florida.

BULLFIGHTING

Since its introduction by the Spaniards in the sixteenth century, bullfighting has become a popular sport in Peru. The largest bullfighting arena in Peru is the Plaza de Acho in Lima.
(*A Closer Look*, page 48)

Below: In March 2000, the Peruvian national soccer team played Paraguay in a qualifying match that was part of a series leading up to the World Cup in 2002. Here is the team before the game, in March 2000.

Volleyball

Volleyball is also a big sport in Peru, particularly among women. Peruvians everywhere, from the jungle to the coast, enjoy watching and playing this sport. The Peruvian women's national volleyball team has done well in tournaments throughout South America. In 1988, the team distinguished itself internationally by winning a silver medal in the Olympics in Seoul, South Korea.

Water Sports

Water sports, such as surfing and windsurfing, are popular on the coast, and Peru's beaches are excellent sites for surfing. Each year, the village of Huanchaco, on the northern coast, hosts an international surfing competition.

Above: **On Sundays, children play volleyball at the massive fortress of Sacsayhuamán, near Cuzco.**

Festivals

Major religious festivals in the Catholic calendar are celebrated throughout Peru. Each village, town, and city also celebrates its patron saint's day with a three- to four-day festival. Each of these festivals is planned by a person connected with the church and known as the majordomo. The majordomo is elected each year and is charged with coordinating the event and raising the money necessary to hold it. In smaller towns and villages, the majordomo's house is open to all visitors for food and drink during festivals, and the majordomo leads the procession of the saint through the street.

Inti Raymi

Inti Raymi, or the Festival of the Sun, is held each year in June. This festival celebrates the Incan New Year and is the most important festival for Peru's indigenous people. During the festival, Quechuas dress in the style of the Incas and hold colorful processions and dances in many towns and villages. The main ceremony is held at Sacsayhuamán, where a man is chosen to act as the Incan emperor and make an offering to the sun god. Inti Raymi celebrations last for a week, with nonstop dancing and feasting.

CHRISTMAS

In Peru, Christmas is celebrated with the family. Peruvian children believe in Santa Claus, although they know him as Papa Noel. Christmas displays abound, and they often feature a nativity scene. The nativity scene is usually elaborate and is built on a large table or platform covered with artificial grass or cotton. Some scenes have hills and mountains, upon which numerous plastic or ceramic figurines are placed, each representing a person or animal present at the birth of Jesus. The scenes have a decidedly Peruvian flair, often including llamas and traditional Peruvian clothing. Schools, offices, and homes often display nativity scenes, and great pride is taken in producing the best and most elaborate pieces.

Left: Colorful and elaborate floats proceed through the streets during the Inti Raymi celebrations.

Left: **Many towns and villages in Peru have a patron saint. Peruvians celebrate their patron saints' days with elaborate processions and feasting.**

Holy Week

Semana Santa (say-MAHN-ah SAHN-tah), the Easter Holy Week, is one of the most important Catholic festivals in Peru. Peruvians have celebrated Semana Santa since the arrival of the Spaniards. The festival lasts for ten days and includes a reenactment of the crucifixion of Jesus. Each night of Semana Santa, people participate in a solemn and beautiful procession, carrying statues covered with candles on platforms around the main plaza and to each of the churches. Secular activities during Semana Santa include art shows, music and dance festivals, and sporting events. The celebrations in Ayacucho are the most famous in Peru.

Independence Day

Peru celebrates Independence Day on July 28. On this day in 1821, Peru declared its independence from Spain, although much of Peru was still in the hands of the Spanish at the time. Peruvians often make Independence Day a long holiday and travel to other parts of the country.

CASTILLO

Fireworks are a lively addition to many celebrations in Peru. Festivals generally feature a parade or procession, musical performances or dance recitals, and fireworks. A *castillo* (cah-STEE-yo), meaning "castle," is a traditional fireworks display. It consists of a bamboo tower with fireworks fastened onto it in levels. During a festival, a castillo is placed in the town square. At the height of the festivities, a lighted fuse at the bottom of the tower ignites the first layer of fireworks. The fireworks pop and spark, and each level ignites the next until the fireworks at the top begin to whirl and spark, often flying off the top of the castillo.

39

Food

Some people consider Peruvian cuisine the most varied and diverse cuisine in all South America. Peruvian food has been influenced by many ethnic groups, including Africans, Japanese, Italians, and even Chinese. *Chifa* (CHEEF-ah) is Peruvian-style Chinese food. The Spanish brought cows, pigs, and goats to Peru, and all play a central role in modern Peruvian cooking.

Peruvian food is varied because the country's diverse terrain and climates have fostered different cuisines. On the coast, fish and seafood are eaten regularly. In the mountains, chicken, llama

Left: **One tradition still practiced in the Andes is the *pachamanca* (pah-chah-MAHN-kah). *Pacha* means "earth" in Quechua, and *manca* means "pot." Pachamanca is a meal that is prepared in an underground oven. Pachamancas are generally large family affairs or village celebrations that require a full day to prepare. Early in the day, a large hole is dug, and wood is placed in the bottom of the pit. The wood is then lit and several large, washed stones are placed on top to retain the heat. Next, beans, potatoes, and ears of corn are thrown into the pit, followed by pieces of pork, lamb, guinea pig, and beef wrapped in banana leaves. A layer of hot stones is then placed on top, and the pit is completely covered with dirt. After about two hours, the food is cooked.**

Left: **This woman is preparing** *ceviche* **(say-VEE-chay), a dish made of raw fish or seafood marinated in lemon or lime juice and served with onions, peppers, fried corn kernels, and yams or potatoes. Ceviche is most popular on the coast.**

meat, beef, and guinea pig are commonly consumed. *Charqui* (CHAR-kee), similar to beef jerky, is made from llama meat and is also popular in the mountains. People in the jungle regions eat a wide variety of fruits and vegetables, freshwater fish, and rice.

One element common in all Peruvian food is *ají* (ah-HEE). Ají is a condiment made of hot peppers mixed with lemon juice or oil. It accompanies almost every Peruvian dish.

Peruvians eat large amounts of native grains, the most popular of which is *quinoa* (KEEN-oh-wah), a small grain that has been a staple among Andean populations since pre-Incan times. It contains twice the protein of usual grains.

Potatoes and corn are staples as well and have been cultivated in the country for thousands of years. Hundreds of varieties of potatoes and corn are grown in Peru. A traditional drink in Peru, *chicha* (CHEE-chah), is made from either purple corn or fermented corn.

Inca Kola

In many countries, among soft drinks, Coca-Cola is king — but not in Peru. Peruvians prefer the super-sweet taste of Inca Kola, a greenish-yellow soft drink native to Peru. It outsells Coca-Cola in Lima and runs a close second elsewhere in Peru. Inca Kola is made from a blend of fruits that are indigenous to Peru.

CUY

A favorite food among Peruvians is *cuy* **(KOO-ee), or guinea pig, which is normally served during festivals. The guinea pig also plays an important role in healing rituals.**
(A Closer Look, page 52)

A CLOSER LOOK AT PERU

Peru is unique in many ways. The fascinating culture and remarkable skills of the Inca helped form modern-day Peru. Other earlier groups, such as the Moche and the Nazca, also left behind traces of their ancient cultures.

Today, Peru is home to many different cultures and peoples, including the Quechua, the Aymara, the people from the island of Taquile, and the Machiguenga, a jungle tribe.

In the heart of the jungle lies Iquitos, a city that combines elements of jungle life and urban living. On Lake Titicaca are the Uros Islands, which are made entirely of reeds.

Opposite: **Street market vendors in Cuzco wait for customers.**

Above: **Peruvians relax in open-air cafés in Lima.**

Distinctive animals in Peru include the llama and alpaca, both of which are valued as pack animals, and the guinea pig, a delicacy in Peru. In the desert, a tiny insect called the cochineal is helping Peruvians become economically successful.

This section also examines how the forces of nature affect Peru. A recurring natural weather pattern known as El Niño hits Peru every few years, causing a number of problems for Peruvians.

43

Andean Music

Music has always been an important form of expression among the indigenous people in Peru. Music originally was a type of spiritual expression and was performed to worship the gods of the sky and earth.

Andean folk music has changed over time. It began with simple indigenous rhythms and instruments. Later, Spanish and African elements were added, and recently, modern musical styles have been blended into it. Over the past twenty years, traditional Andean music, featuring panpipes, reed flutes, and drums, has gained popularity in many other parts of the world.

Andean groups today perform with the same instruments that Andeans have played for centuries. These instruments were thought to represent the gods of the sky and earth. Traditional wind instruments include the zampoña and *quena* (KAY-nah). The zampoña, or panpipes, features a row of hollow bamboo reeds tied together with cord. Each reed is cut to a different length. The musician blows into the reeds to produce sounds. Zampoñas range in size from several inches to several feet long. The quena

Below: Traveling Andean folk-music groups, such as this group from Ancash, often include dancers.

is a type of flute that ranges in length from 7 to 30 inches (17.8 to 76.2 centimeters). Quenas are usually made from bamboo, but they were once carved from llama bone.

A traditional percussion instrument is the *wankara* (wahn-KAH-rah), a large bass drum made from a hollowed-out tree trunk, with llama hide stretched across it.

Stringed instruments include the *charango* (chah-RAHN-go) and the Andean harp. The charango is a small, ten-stringed, guitar-like instrument, with a sounding box traditionally made from an armadillo shell. The Andean harp has a large, hollow sounding box at its base.

In less traditional groups, other instruments are used, including electric guitars, trumpets, and bass guitars.

Andean musicians perform at social events and festivals in villages and towns throughout the highlands. They have also become a fixture in larger cities, playing in clubs known as *peñas* (PAYN-yahs). These are clubs in which traditional music is played, often accompanied by folk-dance groups. Peñas are especially popular with people from the highlands.

Archaeological Sites

Many cultures existed before the Inca and Spanish empires. By studying what remains of the fortresses, temples, and artifacts that these early cultures left behind, researchers hope to understand the complex and wondrous influences these once-powerful societies have had on modern-day Peru.

Huaca Rajada

Near the village of Sipán lies Huaca Rajada, a two thousand-year-old pyramid dating back to the Moche civilization. In 1987, archaeologists uncovered several tombs at the site; all were filled with precious jewelry and ancient artifacts. The most famous of these tombs, known as *El Señor de Sipán* (EL sayn-YOR day see-

Left: Tombs discovered near Sipán were filled with precious jewelry and invaluable artifacts from the Moche period. Many of the noblemen and royalty in these tombs were buried with loyal followers, soldiers, concubines, and even pets.

Left: Drawings in the desert near Lima are so big they can be seen clearly only from the air. This hummingbird measures 150 feet (46 m) in length. Other figures include a spider, a monkey, a lizard, a pelican, and a whale.

PAHN), or the Lord of Sipán, is believed to contain a Moche warrior-priest.

Archaeologists worked for two years to uncover the riches of this site. During this process, they learned a great deal about the people buried there as well as about the Moche civilization. The excavation of this site and the restoration of the artifacts gave many young Peruvian archaeologists valuable experience in handling the priceless remnants of their past.

Nazca

South of Lima, on the dry coastal desert of Peru, a network of huge geometric drawings lies on the desert floor. It consists of about seventy figures of animals and geometric shapes. The figures range from 150 feet (46 m) to 935 feet (285 m) in length.

The lines were made between 300 B.C. and A.D. 900 by people of the Nazca and Paracas cultures. They were formed by removing dark stones on the surface of the desert to reveal lighter earth beneath. The lines were not discovered until the late 1920s, when a pilot flew over the desert and spotted them. They are so large they only can be seen as a whole from the air.

It is not clear why the line drawings were made. Some scientists believe they were made for religious purposes, while others think the figures are an astronomical calendar.

KUELAP

Near the town of Chachapoyas lies Kuelap, one of the largest archaeological sites in South America. The Sachapuyas, members of a group of nations who lived in these hills before the Incas, built Kuelap. The ruins of this fortresslike structure form the top of a mountain, and the walls reach 65 feet (20 m) into the air.

Kuelap is one of many important archaeological sites that the Peruvian government struggles to maintain. Although it is over half a mile (0.8 km) long, only one guard watches it, and three maintenance workers try to keep the jungle from overtaking the stonework. The Peruvian landscape is dotted with historical sites, but the government does not have enough funds to maintain them.

Bullfighting

The Spaniards brought bullfighting to Peru. This spectacular event has since become a popular Peruvian pastime and is an important part of many local festivals. Bullfighters originally performed on horseback, but today, in Peru and elsewhere in the world, they perform on foot.

The first bullfight took place in Lima's central plaza in 1538. The Plaza de Acho, a bullfighting ring, was built in Lima in the eighteenth century and continues to attract famous bullfighters

Left: **This matador performs at the Plaza de Acho in Lima.**

Left: **Many festivals in Peru feature bullfighting by local amateur matadors as the main event in the program.**

from Latin America and Spain. The Plaza de Acho was only the third ring to be built in the world; the first two were in Spain.

In the Tradition of Bullfighting

Bullfights are colorful and dramatic spectacles, and a great deal of tradition exists in the sport. Very specific rules are associated with a traditional bullfight.

In one afternoon of bullfighting, six bulls are chosen and divided among three matadors, or bullfighters. Each matador has several assistants who prepare the bull for the ultimate duel against the matador. When the matador enters the ring, he or she performs several passes with the cape, drawing the bull around his or her body while remaining perfectly still. The matador begins with a large purple and yellow cape but eventually changes to a smaller, red cape. At this time, he or she takes up a curved sword and attempts to kill the bull as cleanly as possible.

Points are given to the matador based on how well he or she handles the bull, whether the matador stands firm while the bull charges, and how cleanly the bull is killed. A good bullfighter is given the ears or the ears and the tail of the bull as a symbol of his or her domination of the animal.

SPORT OR SLAUGHTER?

There is some opposition in Peru, particularly among young people, to the sport of bullfighting because of concerns about cruelty to the animals. At some bullfights, especially those in smaller villages and towns, the bulls are not killed.

49

Cochineal

Not many plants thrive in the dry desert south of Lima. Less than 1 inch (2.5 cm) of rain falls per year in this area. One of the few crops that can live in these conditions is the prickly pear cactus. Peruvian farmers have discovered that they can profit from this crop by focusing on a tiny insect that infests it — the *Dactylopius coccus*, or cochineal.

Harvesting the Cochineal

The cochineal is an insect that, when crushed, produces a bright red substance called carmine, which can be used as a dye. The female cochineal produces the dye. It normally latches onto a cactus, covering itself with a thin layer of white, cotton-like substance. After nearly three months, the cochineal is ready to lay eggs. This is the best time for a farmer to harvest the cochineal because it produces the most carmine just before laying its eggs. Harvesters scrape the female cochineal off the cactus with a knife or a sharpened piece of metal.

After cochineals are harvested from the plant, the insects are dried. Sun-dried cochineals bring the highest price when sold at the market, but drying the insects in the sun is a time-consuming process. Using aids such as boiling water, kerosene, or ash before

Left: **The cochineal attaches itself to the prickly pear cactus.**

drying speeds up the process. When they are dry, the cochineals are sifted to remove any foreign particles.

Above: **Peruvians use carmine to dye their clothing bright red.**

Cochineal in the Peruvian Economy

South Americans and Central Americans have valued cochineal for centuries. Peru is the largest exporter of cochineal in the world, producing nearly 700 tons (635 metric tons) of dried cochineal per year and exporting nearly half of that each year.

Peruvians use carmine to dye their clothing and to add color to paint for decorating their houses. When the Spaniards arrived in Peru, they quickly took over cochineal production and began to sell it overseas in foreign markets, where it was used as a dye for fabric and makeup. Today, carmine continues to be used for dying clothing, food, and cosmetics. It is used to shade lipstick and Popsicles, and even gives hot dogs their pink color.

Many Peruvians support their families with this crop. This industry makes use of a dry region thought to be useless for growing crops and is of great benefit to the Peruvians who live in that region.

Cuy

For Peruvians, guinea pigs are an important tie to Andean culture. For thousands of years, the guinea pig, or cuy — a Quechua word that mimics the sound the animal makes — has been an important source of food to Peruvians. During Incan times, guinea pigs were nearly twice as large as they are today and provided a good amount of meat. Today, they are often the only source of protein for poor families in Andean communities, who otherwise live on a diet of potatoes and rice.

Cuy as Food

Cuy is often served as a special meal during festivals or parties. It is prepared differently in different parts of the country, but it is often fried and served with potatoes or rice and spicy ají.

In rural areas, it is not unusual for animals to be raised in close contact with their owners. Chickens, goats, and llamas are kept in a part of a family's home — generally in the backyard or in a large courtyard area. Cuy sometimes live on the kitchen floor and are fed scraps of food and water.

Left: **Grass and other green plants make up a large part of the guinea pig's diet.**

Cuy as Folk Medicine

Since pre-Incan times, guinea pigs have been used in folk medicine for diagnosing illnesses. Ancient civilizations prescribed medical treatment by "reading" the intestines of guinea pigs.

Today, guinea pigs are used in folk medicine remedies in three ways. All three methods require the use of a black-colored guinea pig. In the first technique, a healer diagnoses an ailment by passing a guinea pig over a patient's body. The guinea pig is believed to contract whatever sickness the patient has. An autopsy of the animal reveals the nature of the illness, and a remedy is prescribed.

In the second technique, healers use a guinea pig to find the correct course of treatment. The guinea pig is passed over the patient's body to absorb the patient's ailment, and then the animal is offered a variety of herbs used in making traditional medicines. Whichever it chooses to eat is then prescribed to the patient as medicine.

In the third technique, a guinea pig is actually thought to rid a patient of disease. When the guinea pig is passed over a patient's body, the illness is drawn out of the patient into the guinea pig. The guinea pig is then killed and buried far from the patient's home to ensure that the patient does not catch the illness again from the animal's corpse.

El Niño

In the late 1990s, people throughout the world witnessed a drastic change in weather patterns. This change, known as El Niño, occurs every two to six years. El Niño is characterized by warmer-than-normal ocean temperatures in the eastern Pacific and along the western coasts of Central and South America. This phenomenon was first recorded in 1525, when Francisco Pizarro experienced unusual rainfall in the desert of northern Peru. In some years, the effects of El Niño can be so severe that weather patterns around the world are changed.

El Niño means "The Christ Child" in Spanish. Peruvian fishermen gave the phenomenon this name because it typically occurs in December, near Christmastime.

The Causes and Effects of El Niño

El Niño is not a storm, but rather a change in the way ocean currents and winds travel across the Pacific Ocean. Normally, winds and currents off the coast of Peru keep cold water near the shore. During an El Niño year, however, a warm ocean current

Left: **During El Niño years, floods are a common occurrence.**

moves down the coast of Peru, pushing the cold water away. This sets off a chain reaction in the natural world. Fish near the coast move farther out to sea in search of cooler water, leaving fishermen with empty nets. In an El Niño year, fishermen who normally catch 170 pounds (77 kilograms) of fish a day may catch as little as 44 pounds (20 kg). Animals that normally feed on these fish also lose their food source, and many starve to death.

El Niño also causes huge temperature changes and either torrential rains or droughts in Peru. Each of Peru's three different regions suffers extreme effects. In early 1998, a state of emergency was declared in over half of Peru's departments. Mudslides and floods had damaged homes and crops, and about three hundred people were killed. On the coast of Peru, hundreds were killed when torrential rains caused by El Niño washed away their adobe homes. Portions of the desert that normally receive rain every two years were flooded. Droughts as a result of El Niño affected parts of Peru as well. Some areas in the mountains, which had already been overgrazed by livestock, were left barren, and now crops cannot be planted there for many years.

Inca Empire

The Inca Empire was already thriving when Christopher Columbus reached the Americas. The Incas possessed sophisticated engineering skills and communication systems, although they did not have knowledge of the wheel or a written language. Some of the wonders of this society still exist, but many mysteries remain.

Incan Roads and Messengers

At its height, the Inca Empire covered a vast area, stretching from just south of modern-day Colombia to Chile. To maintain this large empire, an extensive network of roads was built for transporting goods and troops. Most of these roads crossed very rough terrain, but they were well designed; the Incas carefully cut stones and placed them closely together to form paths.

Every few miles along the roads were *tambos* (TAHM-bohs), or huts, where travelers rested and armies stocked up on supplies. Incan messengers, called *chasquis* (CHAH-skees), lived in these tambos. They delivered verbal messages, small items, or quipus

THE QUIPU

The Incas did not have a form of writing. They communicated orally and used an item known as a *quipu* (KEE-pooh) to record information. A quipu, meaning "knot" in Quechua, consisted of one long length of cord from which many other cords of different lengths were hung. Each of these cords had groupings of knots and were sometimes a different color from the main cord. Quipu readers, called *quipucamayoc* (KEE-pooh-cah-MY-ohk), analyzed the color of the cord, the number of knots, and where a knot was located on the cord to uncover the meaning of the message. Quipus were used to track mining outputs, design tax systems, and send messages. Today, however, no one knows how to read a quipu.

across the entire territory, running from tambo to tambo in a relay fashion. Each runner covered a short distance so he could run quickly without tiring.

Machu Picchu

Machu Picchu is a mysterious Incan city that lies on a mountain ridge in southern Peru. Researchers believe it may have been an administrative and religious center. Machu Picchu was constructed using the famous Incan stonework, and each building was covered with a straw roof. The site features a central plaza surrounded by terraces that were used for farming and buildings that once served as temples, ritual bathhouses, and sites for human and animal sacrifice. A complex irrigation system supplied water to support the population. Despite its impressive scale and construction, however, the Incas deserted the city during the Spanish conquest. It was rediscovered in 1911, by American explorer Hiram Bingham. Today, Machu Picchu is the most popular tourist site in South America, drawing hundreds of thousands of visitors each year.

Above: **Machu Picchu sits between two mountain peaks and is nearly invisible from the valley below. It is one of the best-preserved sites of its kind. The city remains important to Peruvians today because of its role in Incan history.**

Opposite: **A Quechua woman spins wool beside an intricately built Incan wall.**

Iquitos

Iquitos is the capital city of the department of Loreto. It lies near the junction of two rivers, the Nanay and the Amazon, the largest river in the world. The Amazon and Nanay rivers are the main arteries of the region, and villagers travel along them in motorized canoes to buy and trade items in the city. Iquitos is isolated and can be reached only by airplane or boat. A flight from the closest city, Nauta, takes forty-five minutes, while a boat trip can take five days.

Although Iquitos is the largest city in Peru's jungle, only about 375,000 people live here. Iquitos's population includes a variety of ethnic groups. Many Colombians and Brazilians from Peru's neighboring countries live in the city. Indigenous people here include members of the Yagua and Shipibo tribes.

Before the arrival of outsiders, various indigenous groups lived in the jungles around Iquitos, but these groups had very little contact with each other or with any other people. In the 1700s, a Jesuit mission was formed in Iquitos, and its population grew.

Below: During the dry season, pathways between stilt houses are accessible to villagers. During the wet season, these pathways become flooded, and villagers travel by boat.

The Rubber Boom

From 1883 to 1912, Iquitos grew rapidly because of a worldwide increase in the demand for rubber. This period was known as the rubber boom. Many North Americans and Europeans who controlled the sale of rubber became wealthy. These people were known as rubber barons. Rubber barons in Iquitos decorated their homes and other buildings with colorful Portuguese tiles.

Not everyone became wealthy during the rubber boom, however. Rubber tappers, who collected sap from the trunks of rubber trees, lived in very poor conditions. They were kept almost as slaves and lived on small incomes. Rubber tapping was difficult work, and trees were spaced far apart, so much of the tappers' time was spent traveling from one tree to the next. The tappers' modest houses were built on stilts to avoid floods. Stilt houses still exist in Iquitos today.

After the fall in the world demand for natural rubber, Iquitos's importance declined, as did its wealth. Recently, however, Iquitos has begun to grow in importance, as oil deposits in the surrounding jungle are extracted.

Lamoids of Peru

The llama and alpaca are members of the lamoid family. Andean people used these animals as sources of food and wool and as pack animals long before the Spanish conquest. The other two members of the lamoid family, the vicuña and guanaco, also live in Peru. The llama and alpaca are domesticated animals, while the vicuña and the guanaco live in the wild.

Left: **Llamas and alpacas are blessed at festivals, and tassels are attached to their ears. Both the llama and the alpaca are shorn every two years, and their wool is used to make many items. The coarser llama wool is used to make rugs and ropes, while the finer alpaca wool is used to knit sweaters and hats. Alpaca wool is much stronger, lighter, softer, and warmer than llama wool, and it fetches a higher price.**

Llamas and Alpacas

Llamas and alpacas have been domesticated for six thousand years. Llamas are the largest and most common lamoids in Peru and are valued by Andean people for their ability to serve as pack animals. They weigh about 200 pounds (90 kg), grow as tall as 6 feet 2 inches (1.9 m), and have white, brown, or black coats.

The alpaca is smaller than the llama and is valued for its fine wool. There are two breeds of alpaca, the huacaya and the suri. Huacaya alpacas have fine, crimped hair that makes their coats look woolly or bushy, while suri alpacas have finer, silky hair that falls in tight curls. Suri alpacas are very rare.

Vicuñas

Vicuñas are the smallest of the lamoids. They live high in the mountains, at about 12,000 feet (3,658 m) above sea level. These small, quick animals are able to reach speeds of up to 30 miles (48 km) per hour. They have reddish-brown fur on their bodies and fine white hair on their chests and stomachs. Their fur allows them to stay warm during cold winters. This fur also has long been prized by Peruvians, and, during Incan times, only rulers and priests were allowed to wear clothing made from vicuña hair.

GUANACO

The guanaco can survive in almost any climate. It is able to live at sea level, as well as high in the Andes, at altitudes of over 15,000 feet (4,572 m). Its coloring is similar to the vicuña, but it resembles the llama in size. It has dark brown fur, with whitish fur on its belly. Like the vicuña, it has not been domesticated, and it lives in herds throughout Peru.

Las Huaringas

For thousands of years, people have journeyed to Las Huaringas, or the "sacred lagoons," mystical lakes in northern Peru. They seek the help of *curanderos* (koo-rahn-DAY-rohs), traditional healers who cure a range of illnesses and problems.

Curanderos study the art of healing from mentors and spend years learning about the spirits that inhabit every part of nature. These healers were first mentioned in chronicles written by the Spaniards as early as 1653. Evidence suggests, however, that curanderos existed for hundreds of years before that time.

The Journey

People seeking a cure hire a curandero to take them to a lake and to perform a ceremony known as a *mesa* (MAY-sah). Each lake has specific powers, and curanderos choose a lake based on the nature of the illness or problem being treated. The journey to the lakes begins in the town of Huancabamba, a small village in the Andes in the far north of Peru. Individuals taking part in the mesa travel to the lake on foot or horseback. The terrain is rough and beautiful, and only those who know the area can travel

Below: **Many Peruvians believe that spirits live in nature — in lakes, trees, mountains, and hills. Lake Llanganuco is one of the most beautiful lakes in the Cordillera Blanca.**

Left: **During a flood caused by El Niño in 1998, a curandero asked the spirits to contain the waters of the swelling rivers.**

through it without getting lost. Curanderos plan their trips to the lakes carefully so they do not interrupt another ceremony. The journey to the lakes lasts from three to eight hours, and participants often spend the night by the side of the lake.

The Mesa

During the ceremony, curanderos use swords and wooden staffs to ward off danger, shields to protect the curandero against bad spirits, and energy-giving stones. The curandero might also use images of Catholic saints to represent the spirits of the natural world. Personal objects belonging to the participants, such as clothing, books, or locks of hair, are included in the mesa as well. The objects are placed on a table or rock near the edge of the lake, and the participants and curandero gather around them.

During the mesa, offerings of oranges and perfumed water are made to the spirits of the hills, lake, and sky. The curandero recites prayers and asks for acceptance. Once the spirits are ready, the curandero includes the participants in the ceremony by cleansing them with perfumed water. Participants are then offered a seashell filled with a mixture of alcohol and tobacco. Then they take a ritual bath in the lake.

Natural Healers

The jungles of Peru contain a wide variety of plant life, much of which has yet to be classified by scientists. Many discoveries of jungle plants have led to the creation of important drugs used throughout the world, including aspirin; quinine, for the treatment of malaria; curare, a muscle relaxant; morphine, a painkiller; and drugs used in the treatment of cancer. These are recent discoveries for the outside world, but jungle tribes have long known about the healing powers of jungle plants.

The Machiguenga

One such jungle community is the Machiguenga tribe in Manu National Park. The Machiguenga live in villages scattered throughout the jungle. Although they have had increased contact with outsiders as a result of missionaries and government schools, they do not have much access to medical care. Therefore, their knowledge of traditional medical uses for plants is very important.

Many types of treatment are used regularly by the Machiguenga. These include cures for common illnesses, such as diarrhea, headaches, fevers, and scrapes and cuts, as well as cures

Left: **Quinine, which comes from the bark of the cinchona tree, is an important component in the treatment of malaria.**

Left: **While hunting, many jungle tribes, such as the Yagua, immobilize animals with blowgun darts dipped in curare.**

for more serious illnesses, such as snakebites or certain tropical diseases. The Machiguenga also believe that plants can stop nightmares, make anger go away, and help babies sleep at night.

The outside world has benefited a great deal from the knowledge of the Machiguenga and other tribes. The drug curare, for example, changed modern surgery from the day it was introduced; it is given to patients before surgery to relax their muscles. The Machiguenga have known of its power for a long time. They coat the tips of blowgun darts with curare when hunting animals. They also use it to treat skin infections. Aspirin, another common medication, can be made from the bark of a tree found in the Peruvian jungle.

New treatments are coming to light as well. Cat's Claw, a vine that grows in Peru, has been used throughout the Amazon for generations to treat colds and arthritis. Recently, the medical community has discovered that it helps boost the immune system. Researchers are now studying whether it can be used successfully to aid in the treatment of cancer and acquired immune deficiency syndrome (AIDS).

The Machiguenga know over three hundred species of medicinal plants. Many future cures may lie within the jungle, some of which may already be used by tribes that live there now. Researchers and scientists still have much to learn from the Machiguenga and other groups that call the jungle their home.

Peruvian Handicrafts

Peru has a great variety of traditional handicrafts. Each region produces its own type of artwork, and each village has unique creations. The growth in tourism has made these handicrafts popular, so many artisans have returned to their craft after years of working at other jobs.

Left: **This Moche ceramic is believed to be between 1,000 and 1,700 years old.**

Ceramics

The Moche people, who lived in northern Peru before Incan times, produced some of the finest ceramics in the world through the use of molds. Moche ceramics showed lifelike images of the daily lives of people. Today, in the village of Chulucanas, artisans use dark-colored clay to produce similar ceramic pots that are shaped like round-bellied villagers. Decorated with bright-colored paints, these ceramics show the people's daily activities.

In the jungle, members of the Shipibo tribe form pots by hand, using clay blended with tree ash. They pinch the clay to form the paper-thin walls of the pots. The pots are then dried in the sun and painted with geometric snake designs, which the Shipibo also use to decorate their clothing and jewelry. These ceramics are used daily as dishes and pots, but many are sold to tourists.

Retablos

Artists from Ayacucho in central Peru make *retablos* (ray-TAH-blohs), or altars. Retablos are boxes with two hinged doors on the front that open to reveal tiny, three-dimensional characters in various scenes. Catholic priests who arrived with the Spaniards introduced the art of the retablo. Retablos were originally used as altars for traveling priests and depicted scenes from the life of Christ, but indigenous Peruvians adopted the basic form and used retablos to depict their own gods and spirits.

TEXTILES

Peru has a rich history in weaving and creating textiles, dating back thousands of years. When the Spanish conquered Peru, many art forms, including weaving, were forbidden, and the traditions were lost. Today, weavers are studying ancient patterns and colors, trying to recreate them. These artisans use modern techniques and dyes to create their own styles, blending the old with the new.

Quechua and Aymara

The Quechua and Aymara are two indigenous groups living in Peru today. Together, they make up nearly 45 percent of Peru's total population. Although the histories of these two groups are different, their lifestyles today are very similar.

Many Quechua and Aymara live with their families on farms. Their houses are often made of adobe, or bricks made of sun-dried mud, with thatched or tiled roofs. Some live by farming and raising livestock. Farmers may grow one of the hundreds of varieties of potato that exist in Peru. The potato is an important part of the indigenous diet.

Left: **The Quechua (***shown here***) and Aymara have managed to preserve their languages and many of their traditions despite centuries of domination by Europeans. The dates of many Quechua and Aymara festivals coincide with Catholic holidays, but these festivals existed long before the Spanish arrived and were originally celebrations of agricultural or astronomical events.**

Left: **Although they represent almost half of the population, the Quechua and Aymara make up a high percentage of the poor in Peru. Many have been forced to leave their villages because of poor economic conditions and have moved to the larger coastal cities. There, they often suffer from discrimination and a lack of family support. The number of indigenous people who cannot read or write is much higher than that of the rest of the Peruvian population, and their educational levels are lower. They often do not earn money for their work, living instead by trading and bartering.**

About 40 percent of Peru's population is made up of Quechua people, descendants of the Incas. Their language, called Quechua, is similar to the language the Incas spoke. The Quechua began as a small tribe in the south of Peru, but they were conquered by the Inca Empire, which also absorbed many other groups. Eventually, the empire expanded to include a vast track of land in South America. Today, Quechua people live in many different parts of Peru, but they tend to live in villages and towns in the Andes Mountains.

The Aymara are a much smaller group. Most live around Lake Titicaca, near Bolivia, and they are the largest indigenous group in Bolivia. Their ancestors were the Tiahuanaco people, a group that thrived from 200 B.C. to A.D. 1200. The Tiahuanaco society was based in Bolivia and predates the Inca Empire. Their society boasted many advanced forms of architecture, farming, and irrigation, which were adopted by later groups, including the Incas. Today, although the Aymara people make up only 5 percent of Peru's population, their culture is very strong in the southeast.

Reed Boats

In the village of Huanchaco, fishermen ride small boats made entirely of reeds, continuing a tradition begun hundreds of years ago. Their ancestors, the Chimú, lived in the ancient city of Chan Chan and also used reed boats for fishing.

The boats are small and designed for only one or two people. They are shaped like pea pods and are made from *totora* (toh-TOH-rah), or bulrush reeds, woven together. When the Spaniards first saw Huanchaco fishermen in their boats, they called the

Left: **This man collects reeds in his reed boat on Lake Titicaca.**

boats *caballitos* (cah-bah-YEE-tohs), meaning "little horses," because of the way they seemed to gallop across the waves.

A fisherman stands, kneels, or sits on either the edge or the stern of a caballito. The space in the boat is used to store the day's catch. To propel the boat, the fisherman uses a bamboo pole as an oar. Because the waters in this region can be quite rough, balance and strength are essential.

Above: **Women discuss issues at a community meeting in the Uros Islands.**

Floating Islands

In the center of Lake Titicaca live people who have also used reed boats for centuries. Their ancestors were called the Uros, and they lived on *islas flotantes* (EES-lahs floh-TAHN-tays), or floating islands, in the lake. Their houses, boats, and schools and the very islands themselves are made of reeds.

Uros islanders construct their islands entirely from totora reeds. The islands appear to "float" on the water. Fresh reeds are placed on top when those on the bottom rot. This keeps the top of the island relatively dry. These islanders even eat the soft roots of the reeds. Today, however, many inhabitants of the floating islands are moving to the mainland in search of work.

Taquile

The island of Taquile lies in Lake Titicaca, and its inhabitants have a very different culture from that of the mainlanders in the nearby city of Puno. Taquile islanders speak Quechua, the language of the Incas, while most other people in the region speak Aymara. After the Spanish arrived in Peru, the island became a plantation, and, later, a prison. Gradually, the islanders reclaimed their land, and a unique culture has evolved.

Today, nearly 1,500 people live on Taquile. There are no roads or cars, and electricity is a recent addition to the island. Taquile is only 3 to 4 miles (4.8 to 6.4 km) long. The most important activity there is farming. Farming responsibilities are divided among the families in the community to ensure that many types of food are grown. Crops are rotated each year so the land stays fertile. All food is shared by members of the community; none is sold.

Knitting is another important activity on Taquile, and it involves the entire community. Women and girls spin the wool for knitting, while men and boys knit brightly colored belts, hats, scarves, and vests.

Below: **Life on the island of Taquile is communal, and villagers usually get together to eat and discuss issues.**

Men on the island wear knitted caps and colorful vests, with white shirts and black pants. Women wear embroidered blouses and dark skirts fastened with colorful belts. The colors and patterns of the knits they wear indicate their marital status and social position in the community.

Life on Taquile is communal. Regular meetings are held to make decisions that affect the entire community. If a crime is committed, the community decides on the punishment.

When tourists started to arrive on Taquile, they bought some of the beautiful knits, and an industry was born. Islanders opened a cooperative store, where they sell their goods and divide the profits equally.

Visitors to the island stay with families. The mayor assigns visitors to families on a rotating basis, so that everyone gets a chance to benefit from this new source of income. The family often invites the visitor to join them at dinner and may even treat him or her to a musical performance or dance. The traditions of Taquile are what draw visitors to the island, and by controlling the impact of the arrivals, the people of Taquile have found a way to keep their unique culture alive.

RELATIONS WITH NORTH AMERICA

Modern Peru has been influenced by people from Spain, Africa, Asia, and North America. The relationships that have developed between Peru and the United States and Canada, in particular, have an interesting history. Although formal governmental relationships between North and South America were established in the early 1800s, when Peru first gained independence from Spain, ties between individual citizens from North America and Peru were formed as early as the seventeenth century.

Opposite: **Every year, tourists from North America visit Peru's remarkable archaeological sites, such as the Tambo Machay Inca fountains in Cuzco.**

Business and trade relationships have flourished between North and South America, even while diplomatic relations sometimes faltered. The United States is Peru's most important trading partner, both in imports and exports. Recently, more North Americans have been visiting Peru to explore its cultural and historical treasures, helping Peru's tourism industry grow.

Peruvian influence, together with Latin American influence in general, can be seen in North America today, particularly in its major cities.

Above: **American-style fast food restaurants, such as Burger King, are very popular with Peruvians, who readily embrace American culture.**

North American-Peruvian Relations

Relations between North America and Peru have been shaped by the great differences in power and landmass between North America and South America. Earliest relations were formed by traders and businesspeople who traveled between the Americas. Formal relations between the United States and Peru began when the United States government recognized Peru's independence from Spain in 1821.

Peru's Natural Resources

Exploration of Peru's natural resources defined relations between North America and Peru in the nineteenth century. In 1850, the United States formed a team to explore the Amazon River. Brazil refused them access to the river, so the team started from Lima and traveled across the Andes Mountains to the source of the Amazon. Peru then opened its borders to international traffic and set up a commission to map the river.

The rubber boom from 1883 to 1912 sparked increased contact between North America and South America, as fortune seekers descended upon the city of Iquitos and other jungle areas in Peru.

Henry Meiggs and W. R. Grace

In the 1870s, Henry Meiggs, an enterprising North American, designed Peru's first railway system. It then was built by over ten thousand Peruvian workers. This railway system remains one of the

Left: The Peru Central Railway, built in the nineteenth century, was an engineering wonder at the time.

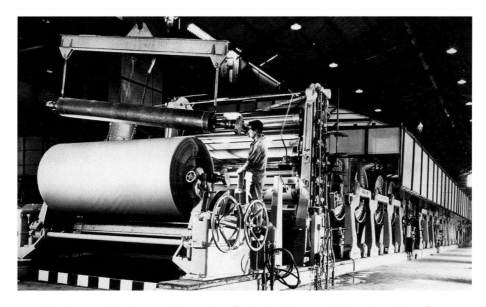

most extraordinary engineering feats in the world extending from sea level at the coast to an elevation of over 15,000 feet (4,572 m) in the mountains, making it the highest railway ever built.

Another North American, W. R. Grace, founded Casa Grace in Peru. Casa Grace was a worldwide trader of commodities, buying and selling coffee, sugar, rice, hides, and other items throughout the world. Casa Grace also operated ships, and the company later founded Panagra, an inter-Americas airline developed with Pan American Airlines. Panagra flights and Grace Lines steamers helped open up tourism between North America and Peru.

Relations in the Twentieth Century

Peru aligned itself with the Allied powers during World War II. Peru's president at the time, Manuel Prado Ugarteche, was a strong supporter of the United States. In a controversial act, Prado restrained the freedoms of Peru's Japanese community during the war, just as the United States did with Japanese-Americans.

After President John F. Kennedy was elected, the United States tried to forge stronger ties with its neighbors to the south. In the 1960s, the Peace Corps program was started in Peru to help Peru with its economic problems. Tensions mounted, however, when IPC, a major U.S. company, was accused of stripping Peru of its greatest resource, petroleum. Meanwhile, IPC supporters argued that the company provided model communities for its workers and that Peru had gained millions in tax revenues.

Current Relations

In 1968, Juan Velasco Alvarado rose to power in Peru and embarked on a program of economic nationalism, which changed the nature of U.S.-Peruvian relations.

General Velasco's military government took over many international companies and industries, some of which were owned by North Americans. These companies included IPC. Velasco then turned to the Soviet Union and other communist countries for arms and key imports. Relations with the United States deteriorated even more when a Peruvian gunboat stopped two U.S. fishing vessels, claiming they were poaching in Peruvian waters. The United States, however, continued to maintain relations with Peru throughout this period.

Later, in the 1970s and 1980s, Peru became one of the largest sources of cocaine in the world, and the United States became its largest consumer. The governments of the two countries are still working together to battle this common problem.

Today, Peru's economy continues to strengthen, and President Alberto Fujimori's free market policies are favored by North American governments. Peru is attracting record numbers of tourists from North America and elsewhere, and researchers and scientists from all over the world are arriving in Peru to study the secrets of its rain forests and ancient civilizations.

IMPORTS AND EXPORTS

One-quarter of Peru's imports comes from the United States. These include iron and steel; machinery; and food, such as wheat, corn, and rice. Twenty percent of Peru's exports go to the United States. Its largest export to the United States is fish meal, which is used as a crop fertilizer. Petroleum, silver, coffee, and cotton are other major exports.

Left: These farmers are harvesting coca leaves. Coca has been an important crop for Peru's indigenous people for hundreds of years; it is used in their religious ceremonies and is chewed regularly by people engaged in manual labor because it acts as a stimulant, much like caffeine or nicotine. Coca is now a controversial crop because it is one of the raw ingredients used in the production of cocaine.

Fujimori and U.S. Relations

In 1990, Alberto Fujimori became Peru's president. He won in a come-from-behind campaign, beating famous Peruvian author Mario Vargas Llosa. In the 1995 election, Fujimori defeated former U.N. Secretary-General Javier Pérez de Cuéllar to gain a second term as president.

As president, Fujimori helped foster strong relations with North America. He implemented strict reform measures to fight Peru's economic problems. In 1992, Fujimori dissolved the Congress and judicial bodies in Peru, inciting strong protests from the U.S. government, which feared a possible return to a dictatorship. Some democratic institutions have since been restored in Peru.

Fujimori captured the heads of terrorist movements that had paralyzed Peru for ten years. He has negotiated agreements with the United States for fighting narcotrafficking, or the trade in illegal drugs, and is working with the United States to encourage Peruvian farmers growing coca, one of the ingredients in making cocaine, to grow alternative crops. In 2000, however, when Fujimori won reelection for a third term as president, the U.S. government strongly criticized the way the vote was conducted.

Left: **Javier Pérez de Cuéllar (*center*) poses with present U.N. Secretary-General Kofi Annan (*right*) of Ghana and outgoing Secretary-General Boutros Boutros-Ghali (*left*) of Egypt at the U.N. headquarters in New York on December 17, 1996.**

Javier Pérez de Cuéllar

Javier Pérez de Cuéllar is one of Peru's most famous ambassadors. He was born in Lima in 1920. He studied law and later joined the Ministry of Foreign Affairs before beginning his career as Peru's ambassador to Switzerland, the Soviet Union, Poland, and Venezuela. He served as permanent representative of Peru to the United Nations (U.N.) from 1971 to 1975. In 1982, he became secretary-general of the U.N. and served for ten years. Pérez de Cuéllar felt strongly that the role of the U.N. should be strengthened so that all countries, large and small, could have a voice in the international forum. He won praise for his diplomacy in ending the 1988 Iran-Iraq War and in securing the independence of Namibia in 1990. In 1995, Pérez de Cuéllar ran for the Peruvian presidency against Fujimori but was defeated.

Immigration to North America

Relations between Peru and North America date back to the beginning of the twentieth century, when travel between North America and South America became easier. Casa Grace constructed luxury ships that sailed from New York to Callao, Peru's major port. Panagra Airlines, owned by Grace Industries, in partnership with Pan American, flew between several cities in the United States and Peru. During the 1920s, Grace Line ships encouraged North Americans to switch the focus of their vacations from Europe to South America, and wealthy Peruvians were drawn away from Europe as a vacation destination, favoring American cities instead. Casa Grace offered discounts to South American students and teachers traveling to North American universities and encouraged cultural exchanges between Peru and North America.

Today, Peruvian students and teachers continue to go to the United States and Canada to attend universities or teach. Exchanges have been fostered by programs such as the Fulbright Scholar Program, which sponsors students and educators from North America and Peru to teach and study abroad.

Immigration from Peru to the United States and Canada peaked in the period from 1985 to 1993, as Peruvians sought better economic conditions and a more stable political environment. Sendero Luminoso and other guerrilla groups were battling government forces in various parts of Peru, and services throughout the country were unreliable. Emigrants during this period included a large number of Peruvian professionals, particularly those in the fields of science and technology, who were dismayed at the low salaries and the limited resources available to develop their work.

Below: **During the 1980s, terrorist activities such as bombings in Peru led many Peruvians to leave their home country for North America, in search of stability and jobs.**

Peruvians in North America

Upon arriving in North America, many Peruvians settled in large cities, such as Toronto, Montreal, Los Angeles, and New York. Some 500,000 Peruvians now live in New Jersey. Vancouver has a Peruvian business association that provides assistance to business people of Peruvian descent or people wanting to do business in Peru. The Peruvian-American population tends to settle in specific areas in part because Peruvians, like many other Latin Americans, prefer to live in a community with others from their home country.

Not all Peruvians come to North America to stay, however; some work in North America and send money home to Peru. Life in North America can be difficult for Peruvians. Many are poorly educated, and they often are unable to find jobs in the fields in which they worked in Peru. Many Peruvian-Americans have to accept low-paying, unskilled work. This is particularly true for those who come to North America as illegal immigrants and those who do not speak English.

INTERNET

With the rise in the popularity and availability of computers in the United States and Peru, contact between Peruvians in North America and those in Peru has increased. A link called Quipunet (www.quipu.net) was started to provide information, gathered by Peruvian scholars and professionals throughout the world, free of charge to school systems in Peru. The intent is to develop courses and seminars in science, technology, engineering, and other subjects.

North Americans in Peru

North Americans are traveling and moving to Peru in greater numbers since the terrorist activities that marked the 1980s and 1990s have decreased. Business and investment opportunities have drawn many North Americans to the country. About 8,700 North Americans reside in Peru, and over two hundred U.S. companies are represented there.

Many North Americans live and work in Peru for embassies and aid organizations. The United States Agency for International Development (USAID) has its largest South American project in Peru.

Two schools with North American affiliations in Lima are the Franklin Delano Roosevelt School and the Instituto Peruano Norteamericano (Peruvian North American Institute). Many North Americans are employed as instructors there.

Many North Americans also visit Peru as tourists. Researchers and scientists come from universities and colleges in North America to study Peru's biologically diverse jungles, its countless archaeological sites, and the rich cultural traditions of Peru's minority populations.

Above: **North American tourists are visiting Peru in greater numbers. Favorite tourist sites include Cuzco and Machu Picchu (*shown above*). Adventure tourism is also gaining prominence, and trips to the jungle, trekking in the Andes, rafting in the deep canyons near Arequipa, and mountain climbing are all popular pursuits.**

Opposite: **Peruvian soldiers, injured by mines along the border with Ecuador, view a web page on mines on the Internet.**

Left: **Jesús Urbano Rojas is one of Peru's most accomplished retablo artisans. His creations have been exhibited in the United States, Chile, Denmark, and England.**

Cultural Connections

The number of Latin Americans in the United States and Canada is growing tremendously. Experts estimate that people of Hispanic descent will be the largest minority group in the United States by 2020. Peruvians form a part of this group, so the influence that Latin American culture as a whole is having on the North American population includes Peruvian traditions. Latin pop music, for example, is very popular, and a number of artists, singing in both the Spanish and English languages, are becoming famous. The Latin American influence can be felt most strongly in large cities. In New York and other major American cities, Peruvian restaurants are growing in popularity.

Artists

Peruvian folk bands travel across North America, especially in the summer season, performing at art fairs throughout the country. These bands are very distinctive, wearing colorful ponchos and hats. They play traditional Andean music, using panpipes, flutes, and drums. They record their music on compact discs and tapes, which they sell at performances along with Peruvian jewelry and musical instruments.

Yma Sumac

In the early 1950s, Peruvian singer Yma Sumac gained great recognition in North America and Europe. She has a remarkable voice, with a range that covers four octaves. Sumac became famous for singing South American folk songs in a Hollywood style. After recording her first album and appearing in a Broadway musical, Sumac toured the United States, performing at sold-out concerts in large auditoriums, including the Hollywood Bowl and Carnegie Hall. She also appeared in a movie called *Secret of the Incas*, which starred Charlton Heston.

Part of Sumac's appeal was her claim to have descended from an Incan king. Rumors about her were numerous, including one that she was actually a New Jersey housewife named Amy Camus (Yma Sumac spelled backward). Nevertheless, Sumac's musical talent and ability are undeniable, and she enjoyed a revival in the 1990s.

Left: Yma Sumac performed her first English concert at the Royal Albert Hall in London in 1952.

PERU

Above: Many buildings in Peru, such as these in Chincheros, show Incan foundations at their bases.

Amazon River C2–D1
Amazonas A2–B2
Ancash A3–B3
Andes Mountains A2–C5
Apurímac C4
Arequipa (city) C5
Arequipa (department) B5–C5
Ayacucho (city) B4
Ayacucho (department) B4–C5

Bolivia D3–D5
Brazil C2–D3

Cajamarca (city) A3
Cajamarca (department) A2–A3
Callao B4
Chachapoyas B2
Chan Chan A3
Chiclayo A2
Chile C5
Chincha Islands B4
Chincheros B4
Chulucanas A2
Colca Canyon C5
Colombia B1–C2
Contamana B3
Cordillera Blanca B3
Cuzco (city) C4
Cuzco (department) C4

Ecuador A1–B1

Huaca Rajada A2
Huancabamba A2
Huancavelica B4
Huancayo B4
Huanchaco A3
Huánuco (city) B3
Huánuco (department) B3
Huaraz B3

Ica B4–B5
Iquitos C2

Junín B4

Kuelap B2

La Libertad A3–B3
Lambayeque A2
Lima (city) B4
Lima (department) B3–B4
Llanganuco, Lake B3
Loreto B1–C2

Machu Picchu C4
Madre de Dios C4
Manu National Park C4
Matarani C5

Moquegua C5

Nanay River B1–C2
Nauta C2
Nazca B4
Nevado Huascarán B3

Ollantaytambo C4

Pacific Ocean A1–C5
Pasco B3
Peru Current A2–B5
Pisco B4
Piura A2
Puna C5–D5
Puno (city) C5

Puno (department) C4–C5

Sacsayhuamán C4
San Martín B2–B3
Sipán A2
Sullana A2

Tacna (city) C5
Tacna (department) C5
Taquile C5
Titicaca, Lake C5–D5
Trujillo A3
Tumbes A2

Ucayali B3–C3
Uros Islands C5

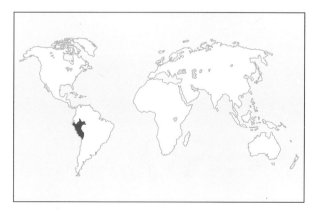

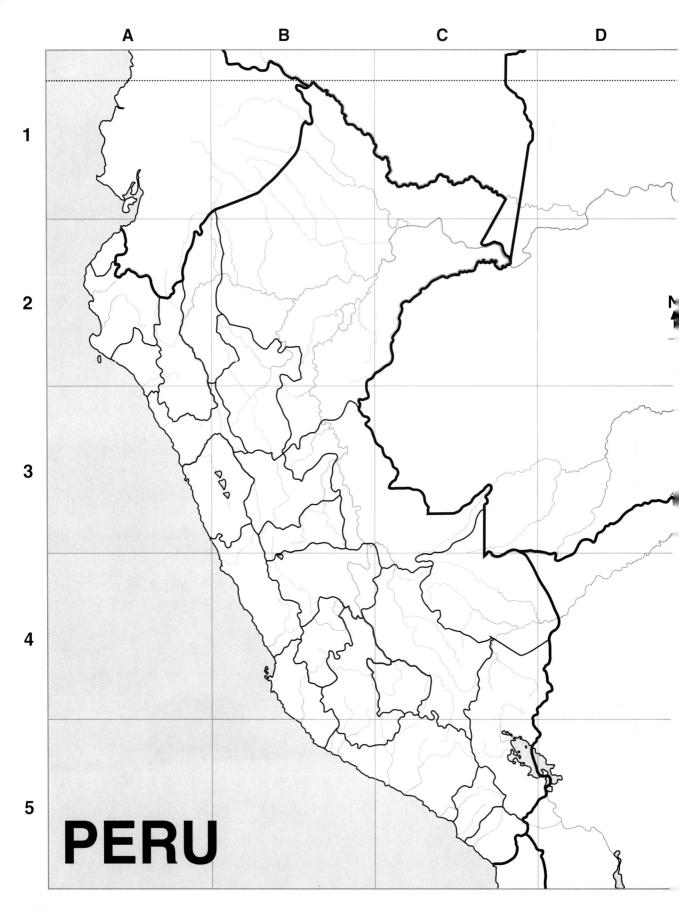

A　　　　　B　　　　　C　　　　　D

1

2

N

3

4

5

PERU

How Is Your Geography?

Learning to identify the main geographical areas and points of a country can be challenging. Although it may seem difficult at first to memorize the locations and spellings of major cities or the names of mountain ranges, rivers, deserts, lakes, and other prominent physical features, the end result of this effort can be very rewarding. Places you previously did not know existed will suddenly come to life when referred to in world news, whether in newspapers, television reports, or other books and reference sources. This knowledge will make you feel a bit closer to the rest of the world, with its fascinating variety of cultures and physical geography.

Used in a classroom setting, the instructor can make duplicates of this map using a copy machine. (PLEASE DO NOT WRITE IN THIS BOOK!) Students can then fill in any requested information on their individual map copies. Used one-on-one, the student can also make copies of the map on a copy machine and use them as a study tool. The student can practice identifying place names and geographical features on his or her own.

Below: **A Quechua girl leads her llama to graze in the fields near Sacsayhuamán.**

Peru at a Glance

Official Name	República del Perú (Republic of Peru)
Capital	Lima
Official Languages	Spanish and Quechua
Population	26,624,582 (1999 estimate)
Land Area	496,225 square miles (1,285,223 square km)
Departments	Amazonas, Ancash, Apurímac, Arequipa, Ayacucho, Cajamarca, Callao (constitutional province), Cuzco, Huancavelica, Huánuco, Ica, Junín, La Libertad, Lambayeque, Lima, Loreto, Madre de Dios, Moquegua, Pasco, Piura, Puno, San Martín, Tacna, Tumbes, Ucayali
Highest Point	Nevado Huascarán 22,205 feet (6,768 m)
Longest River	Amazon River
Coastline	1,448 miles (2,330 km)
Land Boundaries	Bolivia, Brazil, Chile, Colombia, Ecuador
Official Religion	Roman Catholicism
Natural Resources	Coal, copper, fish, gold, iron ore, petroleum, phosphate, potash, silver, timber
Imports	Chemicals, foodstuffs, iron and steel, machinery, petroleum, pharmaceuticals, transport equipment
Exports	Coffee, copper, cotton, crude petroleum and byproducts, fish meal, lead, refined silver, zinc
Current President	President Alberto Kenyo Fujimori
Ethnic Groups	Indigenous (45 percent); mestizo (37 percent); Caucasian (15 percent); African, Chinese, Japanese, and others (3 percent)
Literacy Rate	88.7 percent
Currency	Nuevo sol (S/. 3.50 = U.S. $1 as of 2000)

Opposite: **Fishermen in Huanchaco use reed boats made of totora reeds.**

Glossary

Peruvian Vocabulary

ají (ah-HEE): a spicy condiment made of hot peppers and mixed with lemon or oil.

apu (AH-pooh): mountain god.

caballitos (cah-bah-YEE-tohs): little horses; also, the name given to the Huanchaco boats.

castillo (cah-STEE-yo): literally means "castle." It also refers to a traditional fireworks display.

ceviche (say-VEE-chay): a dish made of raw fish or seafood marinated in lemon or lime juice and served with fried corn kernels, onions, peppers, and yams or potatoes.

charango (chah-RAHN-go): a small, ten-stringed musical instrument.

charqui (CHAR-kee): a dish, made from llama meat, that is similar to beef jerky.

chasquis (CHAH-skees): Incans who delivered messages and small items.

chicha (CHEE-chah): a musical style that mixes criollo and Andean styles; also, a traditional Peruvian drink made from corn.

chifa (CHEEF-ah): Peruvian-style Chinese food.

criollo (cree-OY-oh): a musical style that is a combination of African rhythms and European phrasing.

curanderos (koo-rahn-DAY-rohs): traditional healers.

cuy (KOO-ee): guinea pig.

dar un paseo (DAHR UN pah-SAY-oh): take a walk.

El Señor de Sipán (EL sayn-YOR day see-PAHN): the Lord of Sipán, a famous ancient tomb.

huayno (WHY-no): a rural, indigenous form of music.

islas flotantes (EES-lahs floh-TAHN-tays): floating islands.

mesa (MAY-sah): literally means "table." It refers to a healing ritual.

mestizos (mess-TEEZ-ohs): people of mixed Indian and European descent.

pachamanca (pah-chah-MAHN-kah): a meal prepared in an underground oven.

peñas (PAYN-yahs): clubs where traditional music is played.

quena (KAY-nah): a type of flute made from bamboo.

quinoa (KEEN-oh-wah): a small grain that is a staple in the Peruvian diet.

quipu (KEE-pooh): a collection of knotted cords of different colors. It was used to send messages and record information during Incan times.

quipucamayoc (KEE-pooh-cah-MY-ohk): people who deciphered the meaning of quipus.

retablos (ray-TAH-blohs): altars.

salsatecas (sahl-sah-TAY-cahs): nightclubs that play salsa music.

sapo (SAH-poh): literally means "toad." It refers to a game in which a metal toad sits on a box perforated with holes. Players score points by throwing metal disks into the holes and into the mouth of the toad.

saya (SIGH-ah): a form of music in Peru.

tambos (TAHM-bohs): during Incan times, huts placed along roads where travelers rested.

telenovelas (tay-lay-noh-VAY-lahs): soap operas.

totora (toh-TOH-rah): bulrush reeds.

wankara (wahn-KAH-rah): a bass drum made from hollowed-out tree trunks.

zampoña (zahm-POHN-yah): a musical instrument that has a row of hollow bamboo reeds of different lengths tied together with a cord or string; panpipes.

English Vocabulary

acquired immune deficiency syndrome (AIDS): a disease that destroys the body's immune system so that the body has no protection against other diseases.

adobe: sun-dried bricks made of mud and straw.

archaeologist: a person who studies past societies by examining their artifacts, buildings, tools, and remains.

autopsy: the dissection of a body after death to determine the cause of death.

chronicles: records of a series of events.

cochineal: a small insect that grows on the prickly pear cactus.

cornucopia: a horn- or cone-shaped container, which symbolizes abundance.

curare: a substance derived from tropical plants and used as a muscle relaxant.

denounced: condemned a person or action thought to be wrong or evil.

dictators: rulers with absolute power and authority.

discrimination: the act of treating a person or group of people less favorably than other groups.

fish meal: dried, ground fish used for animal feed or fertilizer.

guano: the excrement of sea birds and bats, which is used as fertilizer.

impetus: driving force; stimulus.

indigenous: native to a particular country or region.

lamoids: a family of animals related to the camel group. Lamoids include llamas, alpacas, vicuñas, and guanacos.

legitimacy: the state of being lawful.

linguistic: relating to language.

majordomo: a person responsible for organizing an event.

matador: a bullfighter.

mentors: people who teach or advise other people.

missionaries: people sent by a church to an area to convert the people living there to that church's religion.

morphine: a substance used to relieve or dull pain.

nationalization: the bringing of industry or land under government control.

precipitation: water that falls to Earth as rain, snow, sleet, or hail.

pre-Columbian: relating to the period in the Americas before the arrival of Christopher Columbus.

quinine: a substance derived from the bark of the cinchona tree, used to treat certain forms of malaria.

repressive: relating to the restriction of freedom through the use of force.

secular: nonreligious.

socioeconomic: relating to a combination of social and economic factors.

stern: the back end of a ship or boat.

suppress: put down by force; subdue.

More Books to Read

Isabella: A Wish for Miguel Peru. Girlhood Journeys series. Shirlee P. Newman (Aladdin Paperbacks)

Peru. Cultures of the World series. Kieran Falconer (Benchmark Books)

Peru. Economically Developing Countries series. Edward A. Parker (Raintree/Steck-Vaughn)

Peru. Enchantment of the World series. Marion Morrison (Children's Press)

Peru. Major World Nations series. Garry Lyle (Chelsea House Publishing)

Peru. True Books series. Elaine Landau (Children's Press)

Peru and the Andean Countries. Tintin's Travel Diaries series. Chantal Deltenre (Barrons Juveniles)

Peru: Lost Cities, Found Hopes. Exploring Cultures of the World series. David C. King (Benchmark Books)

Peru in Pictures. David A. Boehm (Lerner)

Videos

The Living Edens: Manu, Peru's Hidden Rain Forest. (PBS Home Video)

Mysteries of Peru. (Acorn Media)

Peru: Land of the Incas. (Choices, Inc.)

Peru: Spirits of the Amazon. (Wellspring Media)

Web Sites

www.destination360.com/lostcities.htm

www.inter-latin-net.com/peruanos/peruanos.html

www.quipu.net

www.peru-explorer.com

Due to the dynamic nature of the Internet, some web sites stay current longer than others. To find additional web sites, use reliable search engines with one or more of the following keywords to help you locate information on Peru. Keywords: *Amazon, Andes, Aymara, Cuzco, Fujimori, Inca, Lima, Machu Picchu, Peru,* and *Quechua.*

Index

acquired immune deficiency syndrome (AIDS) 65
African slaves 11
Africans 21, 33, 40
agriculture 18, 19, 68, 69, 72
    coca 13, 19, 27, 78, 79
    coffee 19, 77, 78
ají 41, 52
alpacas 9, 43, 60, 61
Amazon region 7, 9, 21, 28, 65
Amazon River 6, 7, 58, 76
ancient civilizations 53, 78
    Chavín 10
    Chimú 10, 70
    Incas 5, 10, 11, 15, 18, 27, 28, 29, 32, 33, 38, 41, 43, 46, 47, 52, 53, 56, 57, 61, 69, 72, 85
    Moche 30, 43, 46, 47, 66, 67
    Nazca 10, 30, 43, 47
    Paracas 30, 47
Andean music 33, 44, 45, 84
Andes 7, 8, 9, 40, 61, 62, 69, 76, 83
animals 9, 43, 52, 61
apus 27
archaeological sites 10, 46, 47, 75, 83
architecture 32, 69
Arequipa 29, 32, 83
Atahuallpa 10, 11, 15
Avelino Cáceres, Andrés 15
Ayacucho 39, 67
Aymara 20, 29, 43, 68, 69

Belaúnde Terry, Fernando 13
Bolivia 6, 29, 69
Brazil 6, 58, 76
bullfighting 36, 48, 49

Callao 16, 80

Canada 75, 81, 84
carmine 18, 50, 51
Casa Grace 77, 80, 81
castillo 39
Caucasians 21
ceramics 30, 31, 66, 67
Chambi, Martín 30
Chan Chan 70
children 21, 22, 24, 33, 34, 35, 37, 38
Chile 6, 10, 12, 15, 56
Chinese 21, 40
climate 8, 40, 54, 55
Clinton, Bill 79
coca 19, 78, 79
cochineals 18, 43, 50, 51
Colca Canyon 6
Colombia 6, 10, 56, 58
Columbus, Christopher 56
Cordillera Blanca 62
curanderos 62, 63
cuy 31, 40, 41, 43, 52, 53
Cuzco (archaeological site) 30, 83
Cuzco (city/department) 11, 15, 20, 23, 24, 31, 32, 37, 75

dance 33, 35, 38, 39, 73

economy 5, 12, 13, 14, 16, 20, 51, 69, 77, 78, 79, 81
Ecuador 6, 14, 15, 83
education 24, 25, 69
El Niño 8, 43, 54, 55, 63
El Señor de Sipán 46, 47
ethnic groups 5, 20, 21, 40
Europe 29, 36, 76, 81, 85
exports 19, 51, 75, 78
extended families 22, 35

families 22, 23, 34, 35, 38, 40, 51, 52, 69

festivals 11, 20, 33, 38, 39, 41, 48, 49, 52, 60, 67, 68
    Christmas 38, 54
    Independence Day 39
    Inti Raymi 33, 38
    Semana Santa 39
fish meal 12, 18, 19, 78
fishing 10, 18, 22, 55, 70, 71
flag 5
floods 8, 54, 55, 63
folk medicine 53
food 20, 40, 41, 52
Fujimori, Alberto 14, 17, 21, 29, 78, 79, 80

García Pérez, Alan 13
gender roles 23
geography 6, 7
    coast 5, 6, 7, 8, 12, 18, 19, 21, 26, 33, 34, 35, 37, 40, 41, 47, 54, 55, 69, 77
    desert 5, 6, 10, 18, 43, 47, 50, 54, 55
    jungle 5, 6, 7, 8, 9, 12, 18, 19, 20, 21, 26, 28, 37, 41, 43, 47, 58, 59, 64, 65, 67, 76, 83
    mountains 5, 6, 7, 8, 9, 10, 20, 26, 27, 40, 41, 47, 55, 57, 61, 62, 69, 77, 83
government 6, 13, 14, 16, 17, 47, 64, 76, 78, 79, 81
    Congress 14, 17, 79
    constitution 14, 16, 17
Grace, W. R. 76, 77
gross domestic product (GDP) 18
guanacos 9, 60, 61
guinea pigs (*see* cuy)

handicrafts 20, 30, 31, 66
higher education 25

Huaca Rajada 46

immigration 80, 81, 82
imports 19, 75, 78
Inca Empire 5, 10, 29, 46,
    56, 69
independence 5, 12, 39,
    75, 76
indigenous people 11, 12, 20,
    21, 27, 28, 29, 30, 31, 33, 35,
    38, 41, 44, 58, 67, 68, 69, 78
industry 18, 78
Internet 82, 83
Iquitos 12, 43, 58, 59, 76

Japanese 21, 40, 77

Kuelap 47

Lake Titicaca 6, 21, 29, 43, 69,
    70, 71, 72
lamoids 9, 60, 61
languages 20, 21, 24, 28, 30,
    56, 68
    Aymara 20, 26, 28, 29,
        68, 72
    Quechua 20, 26, 28, 29, 52,
        56, 68, 72
    Spanish 20, 24, 26, 28, 29,
        54, 84
leisure 34, 35
Lima 6, 7, 11, 15, 16, 17, 18,
    25, 27, 28, 29, 32, 33, 34, 36,
    41, 47, 48, 50, 76, 80
literacy rate 20, 24
literature 29
llamas 9, 38, 40, 41, 43, 52,
    60, 61

Machiguenga 9, 20, 43, 64, 65
Machu Picchu 30, 57, 83
Madre de Dios 7
Manu National Park 7, 20, 64
matadors 48, 49
mesa 62, 63
mestizos 21

military 13, 17
music 32, 33, 35, 39, 44, 45, 73,
    84, 85

natural resources 19, 76
Nazca 10, 47
Nevado Huascarán 6

Ollantaytambo 30

Pachamama 27
pachamanca 40
Pacific Ocean 6, 54
painting 31
peñas 45
Pérez de Cuéllar, Javier 15,
    79, 80
Pizarro, Francisco 11, 54
plants 7, 9, 50, 64, 65
Plaza de Acho 36, 48, 49
population 19, 20, 24, 57, 58,
    68, 69
poverty 5, 29, 69
prickly pear cactus 50
Puya raimondii 8, 9

Quechua 20, 23, 33, 38, 40, 43,
    57, 68, 69
quinine 5, 64
quipu 56
quipucamayoc 56

railway 12, 76, 77
reed boats 22, 70, 71
reforms 13, 79
religion 26
    Catholicism 25, 26, 27, 38,
        39, 63, 67, 68
    indigenous beliefs 27, 38,
        63, 68, 78
retablos 67, 84
rubber boom 12, 59, 76

Sacsayhuamán 11, 37, 38
sapo 35
Sendero Luminoso 14, 81

Shipibo 58, 67
Sipán 10, 46, 47
South America 6, 20, 22, 28,
    29, 30, 33, 34, 37, 40, 47, 51,
    54, 57, 69, 75, 76, 80, 81
Spain 5, 11, 12, 39, 49, 75, 76
Spaniard 10, 11, 12, 15, 21, 26,
    27, 29, 31, 32, 36, 39, 48, 51,
    62, 67, 70
sports 34, 36, 37, 39, 49
    soccer 34, 36
    volleyball 37
    water sports 37
Sumac, Yma 85

tambos 56, 57, 75
Taquile 21, 43, 72, 73
telenovelas 34
television 34, 35
terrorism 13, 14, 79, 83
textiles 30, 31, 67
Toledo, Alejandro 17
tourism 21, 30, 31, 66, 67, 73,
    75, 77, 78, 83
trading partners 19, 75
traditions 20, 83
Tristan, Flora 29
Trujillo 7
Túpac Amaru II 11

United Nations (U.N.) 79, 80
United States 19, 36, 75, 76,
    77, 78, 79, 80, 81, 82, 83,
    84, 85
Uros Islands 22, 43, 71

Vargas Llosa, Mario 29, 79
Velasco Alvarado, Juan 13
vicuñas 5, 9, 60, 61

War of the Pacific 12, 15
women 23, 24, 25, 29, 37, 71
World War II 77

Yagua 20, 21, 58, 65
Yaminahua 20